When God Gives a Sign

When God Gives a Sign

A Response to Objections Made Against Vassula

René Laurentin

Published by

Trinitas™
Independence, Missouri, USA 64051

Quand Dieu Fait Signe
Originally published in France by
F.X. de Guibert, Paris, 1993

Quand Dieu Fait Signe originally published in France by F.X. de Guibert, Paris, 1993.

When God Gives a Sign
By René Laurentin
Translated from the French into English

Edited and published by

Trinitas™
P.O. Box 475
Independence, Missouri, USA 64051
Phone (816) 254-4489

About the Author

Father René Laurentin, a member of the Pontifical Marian Academy and the French Society of Marian Studies, has written many definitive works on Church life, the Second Vatican Council, the episcopacy, evangelization, the Charismatic Renewal and Marian theology. He was a Second Vatican Council *peritus* and is a pioneer of the methods of theological investigation approved by the Council.

He has taught at the Catholic University of Angers, France, and holds a double doctorate in history and theology for his work *Marie, l'Eglise et la Sacerdoce*, from the Sorbonne and Catholic Institute of Paris respectively. He is a faculty member of Notre Dame Catechetical Institute in Arlington, Virginia.

Father Laurentin has long been recognized for his scientific and theological approach to claimed apparitions and his search for the truth. He is particularly concerned with the fruits and charisms that develop and strives to find Scriptural and doctrinal basis for messages allegedly received by visionaries. This he accomplishes with great clarity and insight in *When God Gives a Sign*.

Trinitas™

Declaration

The decree of the Congregation for the Propagation of the Faith, A.A.S. 58, 1186 (approved by Pope Paul VI on October 14, 1966) states that the Nihil Obstat and Imprimatur are no longer required on publications that deal with private revelations, provided they contain nothing contrary to faith and morals.

The publisher wishes to manifest unconditional submission to the final and official judgment of the Magisterium of the Church.

TABLE OF CONTENTS

DOES GOD GIVE SIGNS TODAY?

How Does One Discern?

An Application to Vassula and A Few Others

Apparitions are becoming more numerous today. They are talked about more. Opinions often remain confused or open to debate. Discernment is lacking. To see clearly, we will consider the following:

1. the role and status of apparitions in the Church;

2. the rules of discernment;

3. the application to a few cases, especially to that of Vassula, which has given rise to so much discussion;

4. the Inquisition complex

1

The Role and Status of Apparitions and Private Revelations

How to Approach Them?

"When the baby appeared, the family circle applauded with cries of joy," said Victor Hugo.

When an apparition takes place, the family circle of the Church does not applaud with cries of joy. The welcome is normally troubled, tense and nervous.

The number-one problem often seems to be: *How to get rid of it?* (to use the title of a play by Eugène Ionesco). At Lourdes, Father Peyramale [Bernadette's parish priest] greeted the first visit of Bernadette with one of his famous fits of rage which only he knew how to have. The apparitions that occurred in the fifteen years that followed Beauraing and Banneux (1932–1933) were, in varying degrees, discouraged, repressed, or concealed until the 1980's.

For someone who loves Christ and the Virgin, an apparition would be good news as it is for many good

Christians. Why then this mistrustful, or rather, disgruntled greeting?

A Humble Status

There are serious reasons.

1. First of all there is the Word of Christ, "Blessed are they who have not seen and yet believe" (Jn. 20:29): Those who take God at his Word more than those who see, even if be the resurrected Christ.

2. The Church has good reason to fear illusions and delusions, and the hierarchy is concerned about the authority of seers who might seem to have a direct line to God superior to their own. According to Karl Rahner, that is one of the historic reasons for the tension between the hierarchy and seers.

Moreover, apparitions have a humble status in the Church:

1. They add nothing to the Revelation of Christ, which has omitted nothing essential.

2. They are concerned, therefore, with various events in the life of the Church and not with fundamentals.

3. An apparition, even one that is recognized, never constitutes a dogma. The Church never obliges one to believe. It is a free act of faith.

4. Apparitions are not even among the ten theological fundamentals of Melchior Cano [a pioneer in

the classification of theological studies at the time of Trent] despite the quality of certain messages from heaven.

5. They are not the origin, but rather a risk for the life of mysticism according to Saint John of the Cross, who is severe in their regard, partly to deflect from himself the suspicions of delusions that were directed towards him.

The Role and Value of Apparitions

Nevertheless, apparitions have a very significant role in the life of the Church.

They are part of a universe of signs. Man, who is a rational animal, needs them. God knows it. This is what gave rise to Revelation and the rites of the Old Testament. Christ gave us the Gospel and the sacraments.

The Bible is a web of signs where miracles and apparitions abound in both the Old and New Testaments.

In the life of the Church, apparitions have a significant place: Guadalupe, Aparecida [Brasil], Lourdes, and Fatima are among the places of great pilgrimages of the Church after Rome.

God, who is both transcendent and intimate, does not leave mankind deprived of the signs without which faith withers and dies. Besides the objective signs which are the Church and the sacraments, he speaks throughout history by providential signs or extraordinary ones that call for discernment.

These signs have prophetic functions. St. Thomas stresses that they reawaken faith and *"above all, hope."* They remind us that the transcendent God remains present and near. The everyday signs, whether small or great, ordinary or extraordinary, are a viaticum for human weakness. In this way, apparitions are, first of all, a pastoral problem before being a theological or juridical one.

The Liberation and Multiplication of Apparitions

Why is it that apparitions which seemed extinct in the Church are today multiplying?

This change arises first of all from a juridical decision. The former Code of Canon Law, in canon 1399, paragraph 5, *"forbade books or pamphlets which tell of new apparitions, revelations, visions, prophecies and miracles."* Canon 2318 excommunicated those who violated it.

On October 14, 1970, Paul VI abolished these Canons (Decree of the Congregation for the Doctrine of the Faith, published in *Acta Apostolica Sedis,* December 29, 1970, p. 1186). Therefore it was not introduced into the new Code of Canon Law. This new legislation restored Christian liberty along the lines of the Council. It put more trust in the charisms and prophetic initiatives of the laity. It was a risk, but the faithful have, in general, known how to act with obedience and discretion (with some exceptions).

In the climate of liberty, information took the place of repression. Charisms that were for a long time repressed were now encouraged, sometimes to excess.

In the new climate, several bishops have recognized official worship in new sites of apparitions, and in one case even authenticated one. Bishop Pio Bello Ricardo, the bishop of Los Teques (Venezuela), on February 7, 1988, recognized the apparitions of Maria Esperanza Medrano de Bianchi. They began in 1976 and continue today.

Other favorable decisions regarding official worship:

- *At Akita, Japan,* the bishop wanted to recognize the authenticity as well, but in the light of opposition within the bishops conference and in the commission, he held himself within the limits of prudence and short of his firm conviction.

- *At Saint Nicolas, Argentina,* the bishop, after a first examination, presided over an immense procession in honor of Our Lady on the twenty-fifth of each month with crowds of approximately 100,000.

- *At Kibého, Rwanda,* on August 15, 1988, the bishop recognized it as a place of official worship. The commission continues to investigate its authenticity.

- *At Medugorje, Yugoslavia,* the bishops conference recognized it as a place of official worship under the confused circumstances that are well known.

Often discernment remains confused, ambiguous, or controversial. It is important to make clear the obstacles.

The Formation of Commissions

At the level of commissions there is the problem of prejudices or wrong attitudes which need to be reformed in various degrees.

When authorities establish a commission of inquiry, theologians, canonists, and psychologists (psychoanalysts) are usually chosen. One can ask if these kinds of people are the best prepared for a spiritual discernment of the action of God. A few years ago I said to a Cardinal who was concerned about the formation of such a commission :

Find people who don't have a bookish knowledge but instead those with a real experience of human hearts and spiritual realities. You will find them surely among confessors who are reputed for their judgment and their holiness, seminary directors, novice masters and exorcists. In these affairs, a spiritual co-naturality is important. Of course, it is good to name one or two theologians to examine the doctrine as well as some scientists to define the nature of the facts, but also for them a certain spiritual sensitivity has its importance.

This proposal that is both evident and ordinary has hardly been followed up until now. Those with spiritual expertise are rarely nominated.

These commissions would normally have the task of aiding in the discernment which the pilgrims themselves are trying to make. However, even though, at times, these commissions are qualified, most often they retreat into secrecy. With neither evaluation nor motivation, they are quite satisfied to come to a conclusion with an evasively negative formula: the supernatural has not been proved (*non patet supernaturalitas*). This open and practically meaningless formula is often translated by newspapers in terms of condemnation as if the negation were *"patet non supernaturalitas"*: the supernatural is excluded.

These confused situations are the effect of the following confused thinking:

1. Often the commissions are focused on the miraculous, the extraordinary. But wonders are neither essential, nor primary, nor even necessary in recognizing the supernatural, be it a vision or a charisma. The supernatural is, above all, of a discreet and intimate nature. It is recognized by signs that are rather subtle and which good spiritual guides are able to discern. It is something rare and secondary for the intimate graces of God to cause exceptions to the laws of nature.

2. Often there is a demand that the evidence for miracles be absolute and geometric. This is a second error; for the signs that God gives are usually given in a certain "grayness" which does not constrain one's freedom and gives grounds only for various degrees of probability.

3. For this reason the commissions conclude "the supernatural has not been established" (*non patet*). This expression has two ambiguities:

   a.) There is an unfortunate confusion between a prodigy and the supernatural.

   b.) The supernatural ordinarily is abundant in these places of prayer. It is perplexing for those who have been converted in these places to hear: *"This is not supernatural."*

4. Often the very study of the alleged miracles is, in various ways, neglected. The miracle is declared to be unconfirmed, but without a serious examination of cures which are, at times, remarkable.

5. The commissions too easily hold as explainable things that are not explained and for which they themselves do not have the slightest credible explanation. They simply suppose that parapsychology, psychoanalysis, or rather "the occult" can explain everything. The report of the national commission for Akita (Japan) was quite strange from this point of view. The chief expert supposed that the visionary could be the parapsychological or ectoplasmic cause of flows of blood and sweat that were produced more than one hundred times by a statue of Our Lady.

When Christians lacking authority attempt a judgment, their attitude often justifies the following observations:

• Many say: "I have good discernment" and put themselves on the level of infallibility. The Pope himself does not say as much, nor do the bishops when confronted with the same problem. Since the Fifth Lateran Council, the Councils and the Tradition of the Church encourage the bishops to make use of experts to prepare their judgment, which should result from a convergence of signs. Rome itself was surprised when the bishop of Los Teques recognized the apparitions without having formed a commission of inquiry. But he was the only qualified expert in his diocese since he was professor of psychology and spirituality and former rector of the Catholic University of Caracas.

- Certain people make their judgment from the outside and in line with ideologies or anxieties that make them take the approach that the more extraordinary the event is, the worse it is. It is amazing to see the ease and superficiality with which such otherwise remarkable people pass judgments as :

  - "It is the devil."
  - "It is channeling" (in other words, the seer is a channel of obscure powers).

Too many Freudian psychoanalysts reduce everything to psychology, namely, neuroses.

Overly-systematic people and those motivated by ideologies heap up factors to shore up their hypothesis, most often without ever having met or questioned the seer or charismatic.

Those who are waging the campaign in Canada against Vassula have never met her. Although some of them accused me in terms that I find unacceptable, I did not want to get into an argument with them for two reasons:

I have a high degree of friendship and respect for several of them. I have told them my reasons and my objections. I have left all that exclusively in their hands. They will make them public if they judge it wise or they can keep them secret if they think it prudent.

Arguing degrades. It is not a good tool for reaching a true discernment for a matter that is intuitive.

It is thus without any polemical attitude and on the basis of the facts that I will share my discernment about Vassula. I will reach my conclusions as an expert with no official authority. I have been criticized for "guaranteeing" Vassula. I have never used that term. I simply represent the elements of discernment according to the classic rules. Each person can therefore be judge, and freedom of opinion is the rule in this area. Even when an official authority makes a pronouncement on an apparition, it does not impose a judgment; it merely proposes one.

Thus, I respect the freedom of each person, including the opponents, whose good faith is above suspicion.

2

How to Discern?

The Sources

Discernment is found throughout the Bible, starting with the discernment of good and evil, when Adam and Eve beclouded their vision. The rules for it appear here and there in the prophets. Christ promulgated the basic rule: "A tree is judged by its fruits." Twenty centuries of life in the Church have perfected the theory and practice of discernment starting with the Desert Fathers, the monks and Saint Ignatius of Loyola.

On February 25, 1978, Cardinal Seper, the Prefect for the Congregation for the Doctrine of the Faith, published, for the use of bishops, a pastoral guide for discernment (for which I, too, was consulted); but it was published secretly. I do not know why, for there is nothing of a confidential nature in its four pages. Rome accepts and seems even to desire spontaneous opinions of true experts in the area. In the Roman document, there is nothing that encourages concealment.

Basic Rules

This pastoral document does not claim to lay down all the criteria. We will make mention of certain criteria according to other sources and make note, first of all, of a few basic rules to outline the problem that we want to present here.

1. Discernment of apparitions, charisms, and miracles is never a dogma. When the Church recognizes the authenticity of an apparition, she does not impose it: she proposes it. The faithful remain free to weigh the motives that are presented under the condition, of course, that they respect the authorities and the order established in these matters.

2. Discernment is always a matter of opinion, for it evaluates convergent signs: is the case serious, fruitful, probable in varying degrees? However, the authority of the church does not claim to have a geometric proof or exercise infallibility in her judgment. We should not be astonished by this, since also in matters of science there are similar degrees of probability in a hypothesis.

3. In these matters, the authority of the Church remains modest. She invites us to be even more modest. We do not have the same status and assistance from God. We should not forget the words of Christ:

—"Judge not lest you be judged also" (Mt. 7:1; Lk. 6:37).

Thus we should avoid rigid formulas and absolute statements in the light of the fact that these phenomena can evolve. Even an authentic seer can sin or deviate. We should, therefore, remain open to both the positive and the negative signs.

What are the Criteria of Discernment?

1. Are the apparitions and messages in accord with faith and morals?

2. Is the seer believable? (There are numerous points to examine.) Is a seer:

   - sincere or dishonest?

   - disinterested or commercial?

   - healthy or pathological?

   - balanced or morbid?

   - transparent or confused, bizarre, verbose?

   - deep or superficial?

   - coherent or incoherent?

   - flawed or exemplary both in their life and in their words?

   - and are these aspects in harmony with each other?

3. Are there convincing, extraordinary or miraculous signs?

Apparitions and private revelations can be accompanied by a great variety of physical manifestations:

- signs of light in the sun, the moon and the stars (Lk. 21:25, cf. Mt. 24:29, Mk. 13:24)

- effusions of perfume

- effusions of various substances, such as water, oil or blood

- bilocations
- levitations
- stigmata
- signs of spiritual weddings (rings, crowns, flowers)
- multiplication of food
- extraordinary visions and actions when the mystic is not present
- prodigies at the time of death (odor of sanctity, incorruptible remains)
- and all extraordinary charisms

These charisms are studied in an orderly manner by Herbert Thurston, S. J. in : *Les phénomènes physiques du mysticisme* [The Physical Phenomenon of Mysticism] (a collection of articles from 1919–1938 which was published posthumously in 1951). There is also the monumental study of Joachim Bouflet: *Les phénomènes extraordinaires dans la vie mystique*, Paris, Editions F.X. De Guibert, 1992. These authors have studied a tremendous number of facts that have been verified in the lives of mystics throughout history.

The greatest sign, however, which is dominant in the Gospel and which Christ chooses because it is humane and beneficial is healing, be it physical, psychological or spiritual. This last thought brings us to the following criteria:

4. Spiritual fruits: this is the principle sign, one which Christ stated according to the basic rule: "By their fruits you will know them. Every good

tree produces good fruits...but a bad tree produces bad fruits" (Mt. 7:16–20; 12:33; cf. 13:8; Lk.
6:43–44; cf. 3:9; 8:15; 13:6–9; Jn.15:4–8, 16.)

These spiritual signs can suffice for discernment,
whereas purely material signs are not enough, in themselves, to recognize the authenticity of the supernatural.

3

Application of the Criteria

Medjugorje (1981)

Among the cases that I have especially studied, there are the apparitions of Medjugorje. I have written sixteen volumes about them, and they occupy, therefore, a prominent place in my studies. The events took place along a bumpy road of trials that make one think of the labor pains of childbirth: communist opposition, the draconian opposition of the bishop, along with the inherent problems of obedience. The obligation of obedience was respected. I have studied the historical, scientific and theological aspects of these apparitions.

The evaluation can be summed up in this way: there are satisfactory responses to the objections that were raised despite some errors or ambiguities such as are always present in our sinful world. However, the convergence of positive signs is objectively just as satisfying as the great recognized apparitions of Lourdes or Fatima. Until the war, it was the place in the world where there were the most confessions and conversions. Before the collapse of communism, the Marxist government accepted the apparitions as a religious fact rather than a political one. That acceptance was the beautiful crowning of a message of peace that culminated with its invitation, a true challenge to the Balkan conflicts:

Love your Muslim brothers,
love your Serbian Orthodox brothers,
love those who govern you (the communists).
(taken from *La Vierge, apparait-elle à Medjugorje?*
1990. p. 272)

My criteria for evaluating other apparitions are to be found in other articles.

San Nicolas

At San Nicolas in Argentina, the bishop did not make any official or juridical declaration. He instead took charge of the prayer of his people, whom he guides and enlightens through his sermons while conducting a procession of about 100,000 participants on the twenty-fifth of each month. He celebrates the pilgrimage Mass. During the homily on July 25, 1990, he said:

There is no doubt that this grace-filled event will continue to grow. By its spiritual fruits, it has proven its authenticity.

In nominating a commission and acting with extreme prudence, the bishop has realized that the apparition is, above all, a pastoral problem and a problem of spiritual discernment before being a juridical or scientific one. His example deserves to be followed. (René Laurentin: *San Nicolas: Un peuple de Marie en Argentine,* Paris, 1988, O.E.I.L., and the *Bible de Notre-Dame,* a collection of the messages with the biblical texts to which the apparition refers, Editions F.X. De Guibert).

Scottsdale, Arizona

At Scottsdale, the commission has praised the fervor and the fruits, but it has not decided if all can be explained by human or divine origin.

My own feeling is that, in spite of some problems and ambiguities as in the case of all apparitions, there is an authentic phenomenon of grace, which is recognizable above all by the remarkable spiritual fruits, without forgetting the healings that take place. These healings require a specifically scientific study (René Laurentin, *Notre Seigneur et Notre-Dame à Scottsdale? Charismes fructueux dans un paroisse américaine traditionnelle*, Faith, PO Box 237, Milford, Ohio, 45150).

Santa Maria, California

In Santa Maria, California, Carol J. Nole, the fifty-year-old mother of a family received locutions (not apparitions) from March 24 to September 2, 1988. Our Lady asked her to have a cross erected on the side of a hill near the town. The accomplishment of the task involved a lot of negotiations with the owners of the land. The fervor that arose saw the appearance of several seers as happened at Lourdes where there was an epidemic of 50 seers of all sorts from April 13 to July 11, 1858. Only Bernadette has remained.

But one could wonder about the case of another visionary, Marie Courrech, who gave no grounds for objections.

These phenomena are very difficult to evaluate. They have given rise at Santa Maria to disagreements and divisions regarding one of the visionaries, and that wounded the harmony and cohesiveness of the movement. But the sincere efforts for reconciliation and the relativization of the other visionaries have brought about, today, their fruits.

Other cases

I could continue with other cases:

- *Finca Betania, Venezuela,* has been recognized by her bishop, the rector of the University of Caracas, where he was a former professor of spirituality and religious psychology. It is thus an officially recognized apparition.

- *Cuapa, Nicaragua,* where the spiritual quality of the visionary Bernardo, since 1980, makes itself quietly felt without any official or formal recognition.

- *Akita, Japan,* where from 1973-1981 Bishop Shojiro Ito recognized the event after a remarkable personal investigation, but he recognized it in reserved language because of the opposition in the bishops conference as well as the national commission whose experts were more outstanding in science and intelligence than in their discernment.

- *Naju, Korea,* where there are remarkable fruits since June 30, 1985.

- *Damascus, Syria,* where both the messages and the flow of olive oil at the home of young Myrna, mother of a family, make a good impression.

- *Cuenca, Ecuador,* where the word of the rector of the university, Julio Teràn Dutari, S. J., (*El amor de Dios Triunfa,* 1991) and Sister Isabel Bettwy, I.A. (*The Guardian of the Faith*) opposed the reservations of the bishop.

All these cases are mentioned or studied to one degree or another in *The Apparitions of the Blessed Virgin Mary Today,* René Laurentin, Veritas, Dublin, 1991.

4

Vassula

What you are awaiting today, given that she is here and given the disagreements that have arisen in Quebec regarding her, is a discernment regarding Vassula Ryden.

This is not a personal question for me. It is true that I have a great esteem for Vassula. It is also true that I see her as quite advanced in her spiritual life and myself small in comparison (though she humbly says that she is not a mystic but loved by Christ only for her poverty).

However, though I attach a great value to the conversions that the Lord has brought about through the faithful instrument that she has become, my personal life has not been marked by her messages. I get too many of them for one to become my "cup of tea" or my basic nourishment. That does not mean that I have not read them (as some have said to discredit me; for the opponents, surprised by the fact that I had not "seen" their objections, think that I am quite ignorant).

Though my way of analysis has its limitations, I have made a serious study. Vassula always remains open to information and objections, which I have unceasingly taken note of and examined without being polemical in dialogue with the opponents.

I admire the degree to which reading or listening to Vassula has reinvigorated the spiritual appetite of so many undernourished Christians. But for me, my personal life has been nourished for too long by the basic readings: the Gospel, the sacraments and the example of the saints. So much so that no particular message is, for me, an event or plateau, not even Medjugorje, where I definitely admire the work of God. In this regard I am quite in agreement with Archbishop Fortier of Sherbrooke who says:

> The origin of all true Christian spirituality remains the Word conveyed to us by the Liturgy, the writings of the Fathers and the Doctors of the Church, and the spiritual authors approved by the Church (His critical article of March 22, 1992 entitled: Mrs. Vassula Ryden, 1942–).

As we have said, private revelations have a more modest position in the Church, but they have a prophetic role that is valuable, especially in times of apostasy, tepidity, and the social and cultural strangulation of the faith found in our own times. It is then that God raises up prophets that he has always chosen in a surprising way.

This personal and legal distance that I have is another guarantee of my objectivity. However, it does not stop me from appreciating a breath of fresh air, the transparency, the perseverance, the force of love for Christ and the power of the witness of Vassula.

Summary of the Prejudices

Vassula is one of the most balanced and transparent seers that I know. I would even be tempted to say that she is, in a most satisfying way, more normal, more balanced than most others.

Nevertheless, she has excited more opposition than any other. Why? Is it because she is Orthodox? A woman? Remarried? Is it the extent of her influence such to make one fear that the fruits of her activity give rise to persecutions from Satan? It is difficult to measure the role of each of these factors as well as several others.

- Vassula is Orthodox, thus it is presumed that she is certainly a heretic.

The Orthodox are separated from the Catholics by a schism, not by a heresy. They acknowledge all the dogmas before the separation of 1054. That leaves the Pope and the Immaculate Conception. The latter comes to us from their oriental tradition, but it is now rejected by most due to the papal definition. In these two points, Vassula adheres fully to the Catholic doctrine, and that creates a problem for certain Orthodox people. An Orthodox theologian who had been invited to write a preface for her messages declined the invitation, saying: "It is too Catholic." Vassula's ecumenism is not minimal; it is whole.

Another prejudice: She is a woman who speaks of theology. That is still not accepted by all.

- She is of Greek origin. She comes from another culture. That causes misunderstanding for others.

- She is divorced and remarried. That seems to be the biggest problem. In fact, her marital status today is perfectly in order. She was married in church to a Protestant (1966) at a time when she

33

was not practicing any religion. After a civil divorce (1980) she was remarried on June 13, 1981. She thought, at the time, that it was a Protestant ceremony according to her husband's religion, but, in fact, it was a civil marriage. Only a nominal Christian, without contact with her Orthodox Church, she did not even know that her remarriage could be the source of problems.

When she presented herself to her church to regularize her marriage, the first priest to whom she spoke did not even seem to feel that there was a problem since it was a mixed marriage. But she insisted, in order to be truly in accord with Orthodox legislation. It was then that she was referred to the priest in charge of marriage problems, and it was he who took care of the matter following the "law of economy" that deals with broken marriages in her church. The marriage was celebrated on October 13, 1990, in the Greek Orthodox Church of Lausanne. Thus, according to church law her situation presents no problems.

One might ask, but why did Christ not begin by asking her to straighten out this matter? It is because he has led her progressively, like a teacher, as he has done since the Old Testament. He did not ask Abraham and the Patriarchs to give up their polygamy. It was a tolerance that gradually disappeared by the spiritual progress of revelation. It was thus that Vassula gradually re-entered her church and took on values of Catholic teaching, including the Sacred Heart, the Pope and purgatory.

How Are Prophetic Texts to Be Interpreted?

Finally, the messages that she conveys are prophetic messages, and prophetic messages have, to diverse degrees, a blunt nature, which is paradoxical and led to the persecution of the prophets of the Old Testament.

Prophetic texts have always lent themselves to criticism, but the main rule of interpretation in the Church is that the paradoxes of the free style of language of the Holy Spirit should be understood in a favorable light rather than an unfavorable light, giving the terms that are used the better interpretation rather than the worst one. This is what theologians call the *"pia interpretatio"*: the favorable, respectful interpretation, not one that is negative from the start.

Even the Gospel Needs Careful Reading

No text that is at all original, and above all prophetic, can escape objections. If one looks at them from the outside with a negative prejudice, they cannot stand up to criticism. That does not depend on the text itself, but rather on prejudices that dismember the text instead of integrating it into the orthodox context in which it is situated. Even the Gospel, which is prophetic, gives grounds for suspicions; those who follow a rationalist line and even certain Christian exegetes who cut and tear the Bible into pieces see it, in varying degrees, as a web of contradictions and mistakes ("inaccuracies") according to a phrase that is cherished by R. E. Brown.

Did Jesus tell the apostles to go on their mission with a walking stick (Km. 6:8) or without a walking stick (Mt. 10:10 and Lk. 9:3)? This has given rise to serious objections to the inerrancy of the Gospels. Materially there are contradictions. Nevertheless, the sense is the same: Christ calls his missionaries to poverty without a sack or other items. They are to trust in God and not on human means. The contradiction in terms is clear, but this does not contradict the truth of the Gospel.

Jesus said: "If someone strikes you on the right cheek, give him also your left" (Mt. 5:38) , but he did not offer his left cheek when the servant of the high priest struck him. Instead he touched his conscience with the expression: "If I have spoken well, why do you strike me?" (Jn. 18:23).

Another contradiction quite evident in the Gospel is Jesus saying: "He who is not with me is against me." (Mt. 12:30) This is a radical exclusion. But when the sons of Zebedee were anxious to suppress others who used the name of Jesus, he responded: "He who is not against us is with us." (Mk. 9:40) This is a radical openness.

The contradiction seems clear. Was Jesus for acceptance or rigidity? Both. He excluded heresy as well as compromises with the truth, but with a total openness to love. He condemns sin, but is merciful to the sinner. Ecumenism will not be a syncretism, nor surrender, nor a reduction to the least common denominator; rather it is a common search for the fullness of the truth.

In different circumstances, Christ manifests two aspects of this divine demand, which is simple from God's point of view and disconcerting for a simplistic human viewpoint. This precise articulation of contrarities is misunderstood. It was the cause of many post-conciliar deviations. The Council promoted an openness to ecumenism, but many have pushed forward the openness to the point of forgetting discipline and the truth. On the other hand, others desired to rigorously defend the truth, but they fell into religious extremism and sometimes even into schism. It is necessary to be open, but with control, correcting and guiding.

In the Gospel of Mark, Jesus knows "neither the day nor the hour for the end of the world" (Mk. 13:32); "only the Father knows." Is he contradicting the equality of the divine persons and their unity? In the Gospel of John he says: "The Father is greater than I" (Jn. 14:28). If that were not in a Gospel, it would be seen as Arianism and would be condemned as heretical or even Arian.

In those two places, Jesus is speaking from the point of view of his human experience, that of Kenosis, his lowering of self to a human nature, which is assumed by the Divine Person without a confusion of the divine with the human consciousness. The language of Christ is not that of strict theology according to our Greco-Latin categories, and our theologians have quite a task when working with it. It is not the easiest explanation, but it is the necessary one.

One applies the same rules of interpretation to the Fathers and Doctors of the Church. The Christian interpretation should be comprehensive and well meaning, putting details in their basic context. Christian tradition calls for a *pia interpretatio* for Vassula as well as others.

A View of the Opponents

The supernatural experiences of Vassula began at the end of November 1985. People started talking about her shortly after her arrival in Switzerland in July of 1987, and there were, since then, several waves of opposition. Here are the main ones.

1. The first opponent was Father Schwitzer. He was a director of Father Gobbi's Marian Movement of Priests in Switzerland. Vassula attended the meetings. The fact that she, too, was supernaturally favored created an annoying interference with the messages of Father Gobbi. Prophecies have an impact, and it is not a good idea to mix them. (That is why pilgrimages that try to see many apparition sites in a single trip are open to criticism.) This problem gave rise to a critical examination by Father Schwitzer, based on the hypothesis of a demonic action. Father Gobbi confirmed that it was not a good idea to make a mixture of the messages of Vassula with his movement. However, he did not personally know her and only wanted to avoid that interference.

I have corresponded fraternally with Father Schwitzer. The objections raised seem to me to have an adequate response, and I have courteously explained them in volume one of the messages of Vassula. After that, there was a direct contact between Vassula and Father Gobbi during a general meeting. He maintained the independence of his movement, but after a warm public prayer, he communicated his respect and understanding for Vassula and joined Father Schwitzer (who still maintains his own reservations) in this unreservedly total reconciliation.

2. The second wave of opposition was more severe and came from Father Pavich, a Franciscan at Medjugorje. It was based on "channeling." (This is a kind of automatic or inspired writing that can reveal obscure forces, whether cosmic or demonic.) He applied this pattern to numerous apparitions, including Scottsdale and Vassula.

Father Pavich led an effective opposition with his sermons at Medjugorje and by his FAX messages to Peace Centers in the USA, as well as his own personal activity and that of his followers. Some of them came to admonish me at Medjugorje.

3. The action of Father Pavich sincerely involved two women and two theologians in Quebec who have spread the accusation of channeling by lectures and cassettes. They also alleged a similarity between Vassula and the New Age movement.

This group is supported by Marie-France James, the author of a doctoral thesis (in literature, not in theology) dealing with occultism. She contacted many Canadian and French publishers to publish her thinvolume against Vassula. Although refused by Téqui, she finally succeeded with Nouvelles Editions Latines.

The newspaper *L'Informateur Catholique* (of Montreal) which had valued the spiritual retreats Vassula had hosted reacted in her defense in three successive editions, 6–8 (March 22 to May 16, 1992). Their vigorous, precise responses of a fine journalistic and literary quality laid bare the weakness of the objections and underlying prejudices.

I preferred not to enter into the controversy. I have limited myself to speaking fraternally to the opponents of Vassula. Discernment is an area of freedom, and I respect the differing opinions of my brothers and sisters in this area.

4. I would note, too, that Daria Klanac, in spite of her lively tone and the cutting clarity that characterizes her, modestly limits her efforts at the beginning of her own conclusion:

> This is the result of a research. It is not a question of condemning, or denouncing, or judging anyone. I do not make any pronouncement against Vassula. It is simply in my own personal name that I share with you what I found in these writings that went against my religious convictions and my experience of faith.

Thus, we agree totally at least in this modest limitation. Our different opinions should not be the object of divisions or personal attacks.

Might I add in parentheses that this is not always the case? At the beginning of June 1992, the Archbishop of Ottawa received a discreet tip assuring him that I had been forbidden to preach in Paris by the Archbishop Cardinal Lustiger. (That was an absurd charge considering the excellent relations I have with the Cardinal. Often since the seminary we have been together, and, in fact, he had even invited me to preach at Notre Dame Cathedral and had me as a guest for dinner on four occasions. On two of these occasions we were alone.)

This allegation was made with the hope of preventing my speaking. Fortunately, the archbishop of Ottawa prudently looked into the matter and quickly discovered the absurdity of the calumny. The one who told him was, no doubt, sincere. But that shows how passion leads astray, and this warns us to discern with care and overcome our passionate impulses. Even more, we should ask of the Holy Spirit that these impulses be entirely uprooted.

I was pleased that the invitation to the convention in Ottawa gave me the opportunity to express myself completely beyond any polemics as far as possible, because discernment is neither an absolute guarantee nor a judgment without appeal; neither a canonization, nor the guillotine. It is rather an evaluation of the situation that can be changed by future events.

I was amazed that many opponents had reproached me for "guaranteeing" Vassula with my "authority." I have no authority, be it episcopal or papal. Indeed, the Magisterium itself does not bring to bear its dogmatic authority in matters of discernment. We know, of course, that obedience is due to the measures taken by these authorities for good order in the Church. If the infallible authority of the Church is not called upon in any way in the matter of discernment, all the more so does a theologian who engages in this difficult work have no more authority than the very reasons that he sets forth in his response. It is on that basis that I will present my discernment about Vassula, in complete respect for your freedom and the freedom of her opponents, as well as that of Vassula whose freedom has not always been respected in this affair.

1. DOCTRINE

Vassula does not present any doctrinal problem. If a prior suspicion and an iconoclastic passion have found objections, they are not solid ones, as long as one interprets the texts in their context and in the entirety of the message, according to a solid hermeneutic and not according to the law that applies in witch hunts. It is in the spirit of the former that we will examine the principle objections.

Trinitarian Heresy?

Some are amazed at several passages in the messages where Jesus described himself as a Father to Vassula (January 30, 1987; February 1, 1987; February 17, 1987; and November 14, 1987): *"Call me Abba."*

On March 2, 1987, Jesus says the same: *"I am the Father and the Son. Now do you understand? I am One, I am All in One."*

The language is certainly ambiguous, disconcerting, but the sense is clear. Jesus wishes to teach her the ontological unity of the Father and the Son (co-essential): They have the same essence and the same existence as the Greeks said. It is a mystery before which all language is inadequate. In writing it down, Vassula is disconcerted. She asks again and again. She interrupts her writing to say:

"Here I thought it would be difficult to understand and write down."

Her transcription here seems thus to be incomplete and written from memory. This Mystery goes beyond her, and she remains confused in her lack of understanding and in her frailty before God. She humbly concludes:

> But I feel embarrassed to still have, now and then, doubts after having completed 11 copybooks of revelations. Anybody else would not be like me; by now anybody would have turned into a saint!

Is it not heretical for Jesus to call himself "Father"? No, it is true in a certain sense, for although he called his disciples his "brothers" (Jn. 20:17), he also called them: "My little children" (Jn. 13:33, cf. 21:5). This is paternal language. He compares himself to a hen who wants to gather her "chicks under her wings" (Mt. 23:37). The prophet Isaiah (Is. 9:5) describes the Messiah (Christ) as the "Wonderful Counselor, the Mighty God, THE ETERNAL FATHER."

The mysteries of the Trinity and the Incarnation are not to be fathomed by a univocal language:

- Jesus, who is our brother, is first of all our Creator and in a paternal position from this regard. The paradoxical language of Vassula could be criticized also in many other persons accepted in the Church.

- Paul VI calls Mary "our sister and our Mother" in his conciliar discourse of November 21, 1964.

There is another paradox. Priests who are said to be other Christs and act in the person of Christ, are addressed as "Father". This is quite strange since Jesus said: "Call no one your father on the earth" (Mt. 23:9).

In spite of this clear invitation, there is no other institution on this earth where the title of "Father" is so generously distributed, even going so far as the title "Père Abbé," a double title where the French word for Father is put next to the Hebrew one! This contradiction of the Gospel does not shock anyone, although it does annoy me a bit. There is therefore no reason to attack the writings of Vassula.

This particular aspect nicely complements the language of spiritual marriage where Christ brings to mind his transcendence as the Creator and Author of our days. These forceful prophetic messages counterbalance each other.

The Ecumenical Problem

A certain number of objections are aimed at the ambiguity of ecumenism in general, as well as the particular position of Vassula, for every transition and coming to being is ambiguous.

Vassula has the feeling of belonging to Christ in a manner that transcends the Church, and the Church can thus seem relativized. On October 27, 1987, "Jesus" says:

> It is *you* who have dismembered Me!...You *lamed* Me!...Orthodox! Catholics! Protestants! You *all* belong to Me! You are all *One* in My Eyes! I do not make any distinction.

It is quite ambiguous, like several messages from Medjugorje that I explained as well (*Messages et Péda-*

gogie de la Vierge à Medjugorje, O.E.I.L., 1988: "Objections sur l'oecumènisme", pp. 339–346).

There is a similar ambiguity in these two cases.

At least Vassula adds the note: "You are all one 'inasmuch as you are human beings.'" This unity is to be understood from the viewpoint of God the Creator, who created all things together and united them in a single plan, although the unity of faith is not yet a reality. The message of November 25, 1991, makes explicit the sense of this unity:

> *Tell Me, are you not all alike, made by My Own Hands?…Who has not been made according to the likeness of My Image?*

In the Gospel itself he stresses that the Father makes "his sun shine on both the good and the wicked" (Mt. 5:45), of whom he is 100% the Creator.

Ambiguity extends to the very position of Vassula who was born in Orthodoxy and whose contact with Christ has led her to Catholic truths: the Pope, the Immaculate Conception, the Sacred Heart, the Immaculate Heart of Mary, purgatory, and even to the (optional) praying of the Rosary.

It has been alleged that she rarely goes to Mass (just Sundays) and that the Mass is secondary for her. In fact, it has a primary place in her life to a greater and greater extent. Vassula practices and encourages the adoration of the Most Blessed Sacrament. "It is the greatest sacrament," she told me. "Jesus asks us to receive him daily, and if one cannot, as often as possible." When I asked her if she preferred the Eucharist or an apparition of Jesus, she answered clearly, "The Eucharist" (Interview of August 26, 1989, Introduction to *True Life in God,* Volume I).

She has been strongly criticized for these words about Catholics, Orthodox, and Protestants:

—*"I want them to bend to unite."*

People have said, "that if we 'bend' we will be distorting the truth." That isn't at all what it means. The text is an invitation to humility, to a rejection of all sociological rigidities, which the following words clearly explain:

These iron bars are still very stiff and cannot bend on their own, so <u>I shall have to come to them with My Fire, and with the power of My Flame upon them, they shall turn soft to bend and mold into one solid iron bar, and My Glory will fill the whole earth.</u>

In no way is it an invitation to compromise, but rather to humility and openness to the flame of charity that creates flexibility and unity. According to the context this "fire" comes from God and not from human flexibility. In no way is the truth sacrificed. *"<u>Be the defender of the Truth</u> and of the One Church..."* Jesus tells her on October 7, 1991.

—*"Defend the truth till death"* he adds.

If the unusual position of Vassula is disconcerting, there are good signs of its fruitfulness as well as its ecumenical authenticity. Although she is a woman with no title or official position, she was invited at the beginning of 1992 to the World Council of Churches for an unofficial meeting which brought together the chief Protestant and Orthodox officials. It was a positive and prolonged dialogue.

At Rome Vassula met with Bishop Hnilica, a bishop of the Church of Silence who is close to the Pope and would like to bring her for an ecumenical dialogue on evangelization in Russia, a nation for which Vassula also has received messages. She has visited Russia twice, in October, 1992, and in September, 1993.

New Age

Vassula has been accused of being a Trojan Horse for the New Age. She was dumbfounded by this. In an interview with *L'Informateur Catholique* (April 2, 1992), she answers:

I combat the New Age. How could I be part of it? The New Age means no Eucharist, no rosary, no Pope. And what is it that the messages say? The Pope is the Vicar of Jesus Christ, the rosary is what Satan will be chained up with, and the Eucharist is the life of the Church. This is repeated a thousand times in the messages.

In fact, the comparison with the New Age reveals all sorts of artificial connections between certain themes of the New Age and certain words that are seized upon here and there in the messages of Vassula. The main grounds for these accusations are:

—*"All is spiritual,"* Jesus says according to Vassula (August 25, 1987). This text talks about the presence of Christ by grace. This presence "is not-something physical. So it cannot be explained physically."

This is quite true and important.

—"The Lord is Spirit," says the Apostle in 2 Cor. 3:17-18.

—"The flesh is useless, it is the Spirit that gives life," says Jesus in John 6:63.

On the other hand, in the messages of Vassula one finds the word "era" three times:

—"*Oh, how I long now for this New Era*," says Jesus (December 20, 1988).

Some have remarked: "The Age of Aquarius." But in doing this, they forget the words just before this that have nothing to do with astrology but are exclusively concerned with the reign of Christ who is speaking about unity.

Love is missing among you...I will unite you! I will turn this wilderness into a lake and the dry ground into a water spring. Then I shall place you all in this New Earth...—December 20, 1988.

This is the "new heaven" and the "new earth" about which the Apocalypse speaks (Rev. 21:2). The words that follow immediately afterwards explain most clearly that it is about the reign of Christ.

My Kingdom on earth shall be as it is in heaven. My reign shall come. Oh! How I long now for this New Era!—December 20, 1988.

In *L'Informateur Catholique* of April 12 and 25, 1992, Evelyne Bouchard tells of the conversion, through Vassula, of a young man who had been involved for four years in the New Age movement. It was by reading Vassula that he realized the depth of the Catholic teaching that he had been rejecting. The spirituality of the

New Age then seemed insignificant. He converted to Christian truth.

The accusers then have everything backwards!

The Body of Christ

Vassula has also been accused of having said in one of her conferences that Jesus does not have a physical body, but rather that he is spirit. What she says is simply what the Apostle Paul says in 1 Cor. 15:44-45. "The risen bodies are not 'earthly' bodies, but 'heavenly'. One sows the animal body and rises up as a spiritual body." What is being spoken of is the glorification of the body by life in God. Vassula speaks here according to her own experience.

—"I do not see Jesus with my eyes. I cannot touch him. It is at a completely other level. But I never denied that he has a glorified Body," she wrote me.

On December 4, 1986, Jesus said to her:

—"*Remember you are spirit and I am also Spirit and Holy. I live in you, and you in Me.*"

—"I never denied that I have a body and that he has a glorified Body," remarked Vassula.

Original Sin

The same opponent attacks a particular viewpoint that he says Vassula mentioned in a conference: the soul, at the time of its creation, saw God for an instant before being united with the body. This would explain its longing for God. This opinion does not contradict the doctrine of original sin.

I have only found a quick mention of this idea in a message of September 15, 1991. What is being discussed here is not truly the pre-existence of the soul. Rather it speaks of the initial contact of the soul with God at the instant of its creation. Normally this occurs as it is being united with the body. Under this form it is one of those freely held opinions that there are in theology and which each person judges for himself. It does not contradict the doctrine of original sin, of which Vassula has spoken on several occasions.

The opinion that is attacked here expresses, by an image, the orientation toward the Creator that is implicit in the creation. The soul is marked by the imprint of its Creator: it is in his image. According to Blondel and a number of theologians, it is that which explains the irrepressible attraction for the infinite that we find in man and which is one of the proofs for the existence of God. The viewpoint in this image proposed by Vassula touches, therefore, a profound and classic opinion.

The Eucharist

There has also been criticism of her ambiguous language regarding the Eucharist. In certain passages, it is not clear if she is speaking about the Eucharist or about the Word of God. But this ambiguity has a solid base, so much so that Biblical scholars are still discussing to what degree the discourse of Christ on the Bread of Life in John 6 refers to the Word or to the Eucharist.

Why should we be more strict with Vassula than with the Gospel itself? The same people who criticize her for spiritualizing the Eucharist also criticize her for making it too material (a contradictory criticism), referring to this remark of May 18, 1987.

I have been at 6:30 to Holy Communion as Jesus asked me. In the middle of it, Jesus started talking to me. (Also here she does not separate the Word and the Eucharist). *I received the Bread, and in my mouth it felt like a lacerated piece of flesh which had been ripped off from scourging...It seemed like Jesus was giving me different impressions.*

One of her critics becomes indignant: "This is a denial that the Eucharist gives us the glorified body of Christ!" He ridicules Vassula for making the Eucharist "a piece of meat," "a raw pork chop." How is it possible to lower the discussion to these sacrilegious suggestions? This critic has forgotten the opposite criticism that has been made to Vassula for having said "All isspiritual" earlier in this chapter. Above all, this adversary forgets that the Eucharist makes present and real not just the glorified Christ, but his whole life in its total duration and most especially the passion, death, and resurrection. That is what is symbolized by the Eucharistic miracles as at Lanciano where they have kept the bloody Host since the twelfth century.

The experiences of the mystics are open to objections. The anticlericals know better than we how easy it is to make fun of religion by means of this lumping of things together. Vassula knows very well that Christ is given to us completely in a spiritual way. That is the Catholic doctrine that is so well explained by St. Thomas Aquinas. Vassula knows very well that this experience is not the normal perception of the Eucharist, but rather an "impression" that Jesus "gives" her to show her a dimension of the Mystery that makes present not just his resurrection and glorification, but his sacrifice as well. Vassula has a theological sense that is quite superior to that of her critic.

On September 29, 1988, the message that Vassula receives seems to invite her to take Communion from the chalice: *"My Blood was poured out for you to drink It."* The critic sees in this a contradiction of the dogma according to which Christ is entirely present under the appearance of bread. The text in no way denies this. It simply invites her to participate in the integrity of the sign. If Christ did not just consecrate bread, but also wine, it is because this double symbolism has its importance, and Vassula wants to say nothing other than that. In the Council, many theologians similarly strove to have the chalice offered to the faithful.

2. VALUE AND CREDIBILITY OF THE WITNESS

Witnesses are deserving of credibility according to their worth, their quality, and their transparency. And we have a right to be demanding in the case of a witness for the transcendent, in spite of the theological principle that charisms and holiness do always go hand in hand. Vassula is clearly sincere, transparent, modest and well motivated. She gets no offering for her conferences, just her travel ticket. A reader of her background raised this objection to me:

"Vassula, wife of an international civil servant, woman of the world, tennis champion and accomplished artist whose striking appearance qualified her to be a fashion model in Bangladesh"—Christ preferred the poor, not the rich.

He did give a priority to the poor, but he did not exclude the rich if they were "poor in spirit" (Mt. 5:1) and so lived. Vassula has abandoned all that brought her glory in the world. She no longer has time for tennis or painting. She presents herself to the public without fancy clothes, hair styles, or make-up, unlike Katherine Kuhlman who emphasized her healing charism in a theatrical way: mood music, refined ecclesiastical art, in short, a media treatment for the public. Vassula presents herself the simplest way possible. She radiates what she is and that is how she transmits rather than by techniques or presentation, however legitimate they might be. All of this is in the line of evangelical poverty.

Her life exhibits an exceptional balance. Her house is in perfect order and in good taste. That is something to be admired, given the weight of her tasks. She is able to organize herself and accept help so as not to fall into agitation and disorder that would inconvenience her family.

Her family is a united one in spite of the problems that her unrivaled mission presents with its trips (which, as far as possible, she limits to one a month), her visits, and the innumerable telephone calls which besiege her. She does the shopping not just for her own house (with two children) but also for her mother, who has her own apartment and cannot do her own shopping anymore. These details of daily life have their importance for the discernment of a seer. Here the picture is without shadow.

In the midst of severe attacks that have often raged to have a trip cancelled, I have admired her calm and her balanced humor. It is not that she is without feelings. She suffers, but she perfectly masters her feelings and her impulses. Faced with defamation that seeks to undermine her trips, she does not argue or get upset; she remains above the controversy without rancor or hostility. Her sole concern is that the message be conveyed. She suffers for Christ, whose mission she wants to accomplish, and she depends on him alone. In these stressful circumstances, she does not trouble her friends or force their hand. She waits for the Lord himself to take charge of them, and that is what happens. This struck me most particularly during these oddly repetitive trials.

She has attained, by grace, that indifference that I often advise for seers or charismatics who are subject to hostility: take it as if it were happening to somebody else, or better yet, as if it were happening to Jesus Christ, and with compassion if his kingdom is being injured. I have encouraged other seers to imitate Vassula to reach that same secret of life. Detachment, no doubt, has a natural base in human equilibrium, but it is most properly and specifically supernatural.

When she was attacked in Detroit by Catholics and then at Rhodes by Orthodox who accused her of being a "papist", she had the grace of a total peace beneath the blows of these attacks. She suffers for Christ, not for herself. She cheerfully endures persecution for Jesus. Since she knows that the work of redemption must be paid for by heavy crosses, she is amazed at her *"apathie"* (lack of suffering).

Since that doesn't hurt me anymore, what is it that the Lord will find that makes me suffer?

One is reminded of the humor of St. Louis Marie Grignon de Montfort when all of a sudden all was going too well in his missions: "No more crosses, what a cross!"

An opponent wrote me: "She speaks to glorify herself, not Jesus Christ." Truly it was the opposite that struck me, and it never fails to be sincerely apparent in her messages. In one of the first messages she said to Jesus (March 2, 1987):

After having completed 11 copybooks of revelations anybody would not be like me. By now any other person in my place would have turned into a saint! To his question "Do you love me?" she replied, "You know I do Lord, but at times I feel as cold as a stone! How ungrateful I must be!"

Nevertheless, on March 1, 1987, she said to Jesus:

I am unworthy of all that You give me. I know for a fact when I compare myself to the humble and so dedicated people. I am not proud of myself for having been chosen as the most wretched person in order to receive this revelation. I know that I have not been chosen for my qualities, on the contrary, I have been chosen because of my wretchedness. You have confirmed it, Lord!

This manner of expression recalls that of Saint Catherine Labouré and Saint Bernadette. It is a continual theme with her even as recently as this response in *L'Informateur Catholique* of 12–25 April 1992:

> Why does Jesus accept me just as I am? If he thought like people, wouldn't he have chosen a woman who was almost perfect? Married only once. That is to show the mercy of God. He chose a woman who was married, divorced, and remarried. Why? You can ask God.

She herself is amazed by this; there is no other answer than her humility.

How is it possible that someone said afterwards that Vassula believes herself to be a "reincarnation of Christ" (sic) and "makes herself equal to God"? It is quite the opposite; she is so penetrated with humility that the writings of the Greek Fathers about our divinization by grace do not have any particular echo in her own regard any more than the remark of Christ, "You are all gods" (Jn. 10:34). What she feels most specifically is the sharing in the Cross of Christ (March 17, 1987).

Further Objections

One could never possibly examine all the criticisms that come from every conceivable direction through a nit-picking reading of Vassula.

Jesus calls her "priest" and some are scandalized. Yes, there is a sense in which this applies to all the faithful, even in the Bible (Ex. 19:6; I P. 2:9; Ap. 1:6; 5:10; 20:6). She has never in any way claimed the ministerial priesthood. She herself objected to the title "priest" to which "women are not allowed." It is good to find in her this spirit of the priesthood of the faithful.

Another reproach:

"Vassula's God is pitiful. He suffers, he suffocates, he agonizes. He needs Vassula to carry his cross, he needs to rest. One could say that he has an attack of chronic fatigue." But this sort of language is found with a lot of mystics. Pascal sums them up well:

"Jesus is in agony until the end of the world."

For if the agony of Christ took place at Gethsemane almost 2000 years ago for a limited time, it is in time with his eternal Person. Jesus bears eternally the wound of the sins of the world. Though glorified, this wound remains for eternity.

Vassula is also reproached because there is a breath of vengeance and condemnation. Our Blessed Mother says to her: *If they will refuse it, I shall leave His Arm fall on them. I could not be able anymore to hold it...* "(February 3, 1988).

This is the prophetic language of Our Lady of La Salette. In spite of this surprising expression, those apparitions were recognized.

She is also criticized for announcing the return of Jesus at the end of time. However, all prophesies are eschatological. The return of Christ seems close to her as it did to the first Christians in spite of the warning of Christ that they knew "neither the day nor the hour" (Mk. 14). Vassula does not claim to know either the day nor the hour. She does not know if the return of Jesus is a spiritual return at a key moment in time or the Parousia itself.

She is criticized for attacks against priests, bishops, and even against the pope, though both the messages and Vassula herself show a warmth for him. What the messages condemn are the faults and sins of men, including those of priests and bishops. They are not attacks. They are statements of fact that are more judiciously proposed than the articles in the media about that Irish bishop whose past sin was revealed with such a hullabaloo by the world press. In the message of December 12, 1987, Christ complains:

Never has My Church been in such a confusion....
My Church of today is confused.

Vassula's critics reply:

The Church is guided by the Holy Spirit and cannot be in disarray in spite of the difficulties that she undergoes.

This position fails to recognize the gravity of the spiritual combat. In the fourth century, Satan had overwhelmed the Church with the Arian heresy. In the Middle Ages three men claimed to be Pope. Today, fortunately, the papacy is exemplary, but the pope himself deplores the confusion that is found in so many areas of Church life: theology, morals, abuse of the sacraments, being some of the more significant ones. The spiritual battle against the surrounding confusion is savage (and often hidden away.)

Just as these messages of Vassula give a breath of pure air that converts, so, too, this witch hunt against her is a waste of time and very depressing. These main examples will have to be enough.

3. SIGNS AND MIRACLES

As far as signs and miracles go, I will not stop here to discuss phenomena of which certain witnesses speak: fragrances, incense, lights, transfigurations of Vassula, or visions of the face of Christ, glorious or suffering, appearing to take the place of her own face. Serious people such as Father Frost at Chambéry, or Brian Ness in England, as well as others in the Philippines have been impressed by it. However, no firm proof can be established by these witnesses.

Other witnesses speak of healing, a sign that was preferred by Jesus in the Gospel. However, these have not been the object of a scientific investigation that would allow one to discuss them. Nevertheless, many who have been healed give thanks.

Among them, I have before me the letter of the mother of a little boy, Curt John Dow. She tells of the healing of her son at four and a half years. It took place at a meeting in Missouri, USA, at the convent of the Franciscan Sisters. The boy was a victim of JRA (Junior Rheumatoid Arthritis). She asked the sisters to request Vassula to pray for her son. Vassula was touched when she saw the child struck by the crippling disease. She said to Jesus:

"Do something!"

She touched his forehead and prayed. When they returned home, the child said, "I'm hungry and thirsty," and asked his mother to dress him to go out to play with the children in the yard. She telephoned the doctor for a check-up. He analyzed the blood again. Everything was normal.

"You can throw away his medicines, your son is healed!" was his conclusion. In a month he grew two inches.

In Ireland two persons have thanked her for a healing from cancer as have others in the Philippines and in Florida.

It would be wise if those who obtained healing prepared a medical history so that the matter could be evaluated. In the meantime, these former invalids thank God and witness, like the man in the Gospel who was born blind.

Having said that, contrary to certain current prejudices, miracles are neither necessary nor essential for the discernment of a supernatural phenomenon, for the supernatural is not of itself the extraordinary, the marvelous, nor the exceptional; it is the transformation of hearts by the divine life, that is to say, by love: the love which God gives. The palpable splendor of a miracle is just a very particular form of the supernatural, and in this area there are, so far, only statements without scientific proof as far as Vassula is concerned.

4. SPIRITUAL FRUITS

According to Christ, the principal criterion for discernment is the fruits. It so happens that it was precisely the fruits that first interested me in Vassula. At the beginning of 1989, I had met, by chance, quite a variety of people who had rediscovered their faith and fervor through reading or listening to these messages on cassettes. I telephoned Vassula to understand better. Afterwards, I met some of those who had been converted through her when I was in Ireland and then in Switzerland. When they can, they love to come along with her on these apostolic journeys. Her influence encourages them. During her trip in Ireland in November 1991, there were a dozen of them from eight or nine different nationalities, from different social and cultural backgrounds, and of very different ages. Among them a seven-foot basketball player stood out. Their trip was not a tour; it was for prayer. During the trip, on Friday, all of them fasted on bread and water with good humor and perfect harmony.

I passed a day with these new friends of Vassula during February when there was a meeting in Switzerland: there was a fervent Mass at one of their homes. There were at least twenty there. Then, with ten of them, we relaxed and went skiing in the mountains. In these different circumstances, I appreciated the depth of their faith and prayer and their thanksgiving. All of them had undergone a genuine conversion and radiated happiness. Very few priests get as many conversions as Vassula. The Spirit blows where he wills.

There are other convergent signs on her behalf. In 1990–1991, Vassula was invited to share the Passion of Christ on Fridays around three in the afternoon. Her experience is like that of the stigmatics, which is more common than people imagine. She experiences the suffering and the death of Christ but without external physical signs. I was once a witness. She suffers very much, but there is nothing theatrical or affected. On the contrary, it is with great dignity, with no apprehension beforehand, nor falling back on herself afterwards. During that time she is absent, as it were, living the Passion.

It is an ecstasy, a disconnection with the outer world, but a painful experience.

Besides the positive indications that I have methodically gathered here, first hand knowledge makes clear the Christian simplicity or lack of it, and this has its importance. That is why it amazes me that most of the opponents of Vassula base their attacks on her writings without knowing her personally or ever having met her.

To give an example, one of the reactions that struck me during our first meeting was this. I asked her how long these apparitions were going to go on. She said to me:

> Until the end of my days. Jesus told me: "Till the end!" I told him, "Hurry up!"

She has no fear of death. On the contrary, she desires it, but she remains ready to continue to live as long as Jesus wants to make use of her for unity.

Her reaction recalls that of many authentic seers that I have checked or tried to catch on this point. The meeting with Christ and Our Blessed Mother makes this passing world pale to insignificance; an apparition is not the beatific vision; it is a palpable communication, incomplete, and partial, but that is enough to make them long for the world beyond, which for many others creates anxiety and fear.

5. THE OBJECTION TO CHANNELING

The fact that Vassula wrote her first messages by movement in the hand causes some to accuse her of channeling (from the word "channel" indicating an ambiguous communication with unknown or demonic powers) or automatic writing (of subjective origin).

Before this objection was raised against her, I had brought up this difficulty in my interview of August 26, 1989:

—"But doesn't that change you into a robot? (…)

—"Jesus has told me and clearly shown me that this handwriting is not automatic writing, as some people imagine. One day he told me, 'Today you will write My message with your handwriting, so that those who have not truly understood this grace that I am granting to you can understand; realize that I have also given you the grace to hear My Voice. Allow me today to dictate only. You listen and write.'" ("A Meeting with Vassula," *True Life in God*, Volume I).

—"In the beginning, during the period of purification, I used to receive the messages from the angel only through a movement of the hand. Jesus taught me how to hear him," she added. "It is dictated to the hearing," she specifies.

We are dealing here with a personal relationship that is essentially Christian and leads to prayer, the cross and the sacraments.

The opponents of Vassula have found ways of seizing upon some apparently effective objections from the expertise that I had requested from the graphologist A. Muenier, an expert in handwriting at the Court of Appeals of Paris. He died in 1991. This specialist was of a very high caliber and found in the long, upright, clear handwriting, when her hand is used by the Lord, an "extraordinary telluric force that goes beyond herself."

The adversaries conclude: "What he really meant to say was that it is an abstract, impersonal, obscure force."

The abstract language of Muenier arises from the fact that he only knew the writings themselves (the small normal handwriting of Vassula and the large handwriting under guidance). However, he knew nothing of the phenomenon. He only knew that the small handwriting was that of a 47-year-old woman. He had quite a task to reach the opinion that the large handwriting could be of the same hand, something that he regarded as only probable, due to the formal differences that were there. He did not know English and so he received no clues from the content. That is why he used abstract terms like "the force," the "fullness," and the "tranquil enthusiasm" of this handwriting which is "a bit unusual from an ordinary point of view."

His astonishing analysis identified the unique position of the writer though he knew nothing about her:

> She is an intermediary, like a center of transmission and amplification...very redoubled, nourished by an invisible force that seems indestructible.

While perceiving this motion is of a superior order, he describes well the attitude of Vassula during dictation:

- She is very hard-working; she is a docile pupil.

- She is in a kind of second state, indifferent to the exterior world.

- She does not belong to herself.

As far as Vassula's personality is revealed in her own handwriting, this expert, whose depth of analysis I have often admired, especially makes these observations:

- She is a person who lives in her own world. (by which he means she is not deluded)

- She is not mentally ill.

- She is of at least above average intelligence.

- She is tender, kind, docile.

- She experiences an inspiration from a high level.

- Her life is inspired by an ideal.

- She is simple and direct…she has a great sincerity, and is without pretense.

- Her temperament is very well balanced. Her personality seems to dominate very well her physical state. Her emotional balance seems excellent.

- She is simple and candid…She is serious without being tense.

- She is not easily affected by events, but has a high level of sensitivity. Perhaps at times there is a possible touch of playfulness or pleasant imaginativeness for recreation.

- Her moral level is excellent. She has a firm conviction in her beliefs. Her will is calm.

- She has dignity and also a very notable goodwill.

Some other notable qualities are:

- She has a certain reserve in relation to the phenomena that are affecting her.... She has a lot more than just a "rich subconscious."

These last words exclude automatic writing which arises from the subconscious. It is strange to see how four or five words on this penetrating analysis have been seized in their opposite meaning to shore up the theory of channeling. Muenier, who very cautiously spoke about the unknown, perceived very well that genuine phenomenon.

Briefly then, if the first experiences of Vassula had, at times, the aspect of constraint during the period of purification or when she had her little combat, like Jacob, with messages that were too demanding for her, (as for example, when Jesus encouraged her to go to confession,) she remained free (A Meeting with Vassula, *True Life in God*, Volume 1). She could not write the opposite, but she could stop writing.

These rare moments of resistance revealed to her the divine will to which she would again adhere quite quickly with the love that is at the heart of all these messages: the love of God. Vassula adds, "This force which held my hand, encouraged me and helped to overcome the doubts that came to me from time to time." This absolute relationship is with Jesus alone, the Jesus of the Scriptures and of the sacraments. This puts us a thousand miles away from automatic writing and channeling. We are not in the dark; we are in the light of faith with all its spiritual consequences.

After putting his graphological analysis in terms of force and influence (where people have tried to see the phenomenon of channeling), Muenier was very interested both in finding out about the experience that underlay these disconcerting writings as well as in grasping their personal and spiritual dimension, which was quite different than the odd ideas which people have drawn from his analysis. He immediately understood the mysterious character of this writing, and, after analyzing them from outside, groping along, he immediately went down to the foundation, the inner dimension. The interpretation of this as channeling is thus completely foreign to the spiritual life of Vassula as well as her personal union with Christ and her loving service to God and mankind.

The Language of Love

People have greatly criticized Vassula for having written down her loving dialogues with Christ. It is seen as superficial sentimentalism, an indecent tryst. Vassula, who radiates modesty and tact, would have preferred to keep these dialogues for herself. She published them in obedience to Him who speaks.

The language of love is vulnerable and easily ridiculed.

But this is the language of mystics, often inspired by the Song of Songs, where certain Bible scholars prefer to see (not without reasons) an erotic rather than a symbolic hymn: "Let him kiss me with the kisses of his mouth" (Sg 1:2). From this standpoint, Vassula's writings cannot be criticized. Theyhave nothing erotic in them. Her language is more modest than that of Saint Bridget, Saint Catherine of Siena, or Saint John of the Cross.

It would be correct here to take note of the reserve and modesty of this woman who keeps in their respective places her earthly marriage and the divine marriage with Christ to which every soul is called. It is a transcendent, spiritual love ("all is spiritual" she writes). The love of God and the love of Christ, who is God, is the greatest love there is, and it is normal that it expresses itself in the loving language of these messages as with so many other mystics. Jesus only kisses "on the forehead" as a Father, and she accepts it with infinite respect.

The dialogue of love that astonishes our extremely traditional attitudes could no doubt have been expanded upon by other private passages that have not been printed. But if cuts were made, the critics would have been even more vehement. Vassula has been accused of hiding numerous things, just as she is accused of "camouflaging" some rare omissions from the manuscript version (photocopied many times) and the printed text. But whatever she omitted was done, as with the rest, at the request of Jesus who asked her not to print a few passages of a private nature.

In any case, she knows that she is nothing and that it is the love of Christ which has chosen her for her weakness and even for her wretchedness.

Conclusion

The signs that appear in the life of Vassula, in the messages and in their fruits, show a beautiful transparency of Christ alone. Her journey of unconditional love gives no grounds for other objections save those that arise from suspicion or from jealousy before this experience of the love of God. This polemical ridicule denigrates what is for Vassula solely the cause of Christ.

The discernment of this case seemed to me unusually positive in the light of her human and spiritual equilibrium and the deep union she experiences between the joy of loving and, at the same time, peace in suffering, accepted with abandonment: participation in the sorrow of the cross and persecutions from opponents.

At each stage since my first contacts in 1989, the development of Vassula has simply provided new signs that favor her authenticity. I am even more sure today that this is a grace for her, for the Church and for unity.

This discernment remains conscious of the humility about which Vassula herself is aware. There is an openness to the future where it will always be necessary to conquer temptations and traps of the devil. The objective esteem that I have for her I do not mean to impose on others, but I propose it to the liberty of each one, based solely on the objective signs that have been proposed, to which I would add my own intuitive perception, which cannot be completely expressed, but which has its importance in the discernment of seers.

It is not a personal question. However, I do note to what point reading and hearing Vassula has given a new force to the spiritual appetite of so many under-nourished Christians today.

My life has been based, for too long a time, on the Gospel, the sacraments, and the examples of the saints for any particular message to become, for me, a new event or phase, even Medjugorje where I so much admire the work of God. This personal detachment is an additional guarantee of my objectivity. That does not stop me, however, from appreciating the breath of pure air, the transparency, the wave of love for Christ revealed here that constitutes, for me, a marvelous testimony so astonishingly different among so many others.

Four Centuries After Galileo The Inquisitorial Complex Is Still Not Dead

Why?

Some Comments on the Most Recent Objections

Christianity is charity, communion, unity and that is the way it often is, despite the interferences of spiritual combat. Why, then, is it that we see so often the appearance of divisions and arguments between Christians, above all, between good Christians? Why do they become such vigorous accusers? Even the wonderful Pope that the Lord has given us is the target of a whole ultra-progressive intelligentsia, composed, to a large degree, of priests, while certain traditionalists almost go so far as to excommunicate him.

The response is this: the Inquisition is dead, but the inquisitorial complex lives on. It rises often where no one was expecting it. Why?

1. An Analysis of the Complex

The men of the Inquisition were sincere, virtuous, and religious. The Christians who, today, set themselves up as judges of other Christians, are as pure and zealous as Torquemada [one of the more famous Spanish Inquisitors].

Their firm intention is to defend the purity of the faith and practice Christian discernment. They should know how to distinguish the wheat from the tares. Such a task is needed in this hour of so many deviations and degradations of faith. But why is it that they so easily miss the target?

According to its etymology, the word "inquisitor" means "investigator". It touches most precisely on seeking out error to condemn it. He who seeks finds. Those who seek too zealously for error invent it and project it onto their target. That is the paradoxical illusion of the experts in heresy of whom Voltaire said:

—A meek and gentle inquisitor, with crucifix in hand, into the fire, for charity, throws his fellow man.
(Poem on the Natural Law, III)

What is often lacking in inquisitors is respect and understanding for other people. They see every difference as a deviation or heresy. A trifling matter, and they burst into action and use any pretext to justify their condemnation. They become radically opposed to their presumed adversaries as if they were like *leo rugiens quaerens quem devoret:* "a roaring lion seeking someone to devour" (as it says in Compline).

The virus that corrupts these undertakings for doctrinal purification is often the systematic spirit.

The inquisitor is sure of himself. He often says:

—I have discernment.

He satisfies himself with this certitude instead of opening himself to the voice of the Holy Spirit. He forgets the word of the Gospel: "Judge not, lest you be judged" (Mt. 7:1).

By accusing his victims, he becomes puffed up and glories in his own justice.

The inquisitor is like a soldier who misses the war during times of peace. He instinctively goes looking for one. He enjoys discovering heresy like a hunter, looking for his prey.

It is fine to believe in spiritual combat, but it is wrong to spread artificial wars. I say "spread" because FAX machines today send instantly around the world trumped up charges that the new inquisitors unscrupulously spread around the world. In this way, they stir up and mobilize other inquisitors who exchange and go over these ideas like children who keep stealing the same gum from each other for yet another chewing!

How can good Christians, in good faith, let themselves be deceived in this way? The answer is that the devil is a great deceiver and loves nothing better than sowing confusion and conflicts to tear into pieces the body of Christ and put the servants of Christ's kingdom in opposition to each other. Once this process has begun, the judges are so taken up with their argument against their opponents that they fail to exercise that discernment over themselves which should have priority.

It is tragic that zealous Christians fail to choose better targets for their spiritual combat, for while they unleash their attacks on innocent victims, there are errors and prejudices which lower the level of faith and morals and gallop merrily along without contradiction, even in theology departments where, at times, a deviant professor is awarded a martyr's crown. The arrows are reserved, instead, for the fervent Christians who are concerned with God alone, especially if they are women. For the inquisitor, all Christian women are seen as witches waiting to be revealed. It is his role to unmask them.

The inquisitors have subtle minds and are untiring. Unfortunately, if they read a text, it is not for the sake of understanding or reaching its depths; they are just looking for the weak point, the ambiguity, the bold statement that will be quickly interpreted in the worst sense possible and not in the best, which is often found in the context itself. They pore over the text while avoiding any first-hand knowledge of the person whose life is often transparent and radiant even beneath the violent persecutions which they themselves have unleashed. A fraternal meeting would inhibit their cutting style.

2. Misleading Charges

It is necessary to illustrate this analysis by a few examples from the most recent attacks against Vassula. We will do it without criticizing anyone or naming these well-intentioned inquisitors whose normal behavior is above suspicion. In my respect for them I am deeply sorry to see how this ridiculous debate has degraded them.

Scorn for Confession?

One of the criticisms of Vassula is that she does not go to confession, for Christ himself invited her to confess to him alone, going directly to the top.

Yes, each day she makes her examination of conscience before the face of the Lord and confesses to him. But this internal confession does not prevent her from regularly confessing to Father Nicolas [de Flue], a Capuchin from Bulle, in Canton Fribourg.

According to her accusers she has destroyed the messages she received during the first months, no doubt to conceal the clumsy and shameful errors that they contained.

In fact, Vassula has destroyed nothing at all, except for a few personal messages which concern only herself. She has kept the first messages which began her Christian education. However, for the time being, she has not yet published them. She plans on doing it later. These messages were read and examined by her spiritual director in Bangladesh, Father James Fannan, P.I.M.E. a priest of noteworthy intelligence, humility and discernment, who made her pass through rough and disconcerting trials.

Some people criticize Vassula for minor omissions in the printed version or try to find in omitted words a wrong meaning.

These rare omissions arise simply from the fact that the first people with whom Vassula shared these messages took them and photocopied them as they were. But Christ himself invited Vassula to discern what was private and personal and what was destined for the public. She therefore made this selection for the printed edition. She hasn't hidden anything, given the fact that the first photocopies are still in existence and circulate freely to provide fodder for the suspicion of her inquisitors.

Prolonged Automatic Writing

Her accusers ask why it is that "after four or five years of automatic writing, Vassula has passed to audible dictation?"

As a matter of fact, she learned to hear Christ already *in 1986,* in the first year, not after four or five years. Her handwriting was never "automatic" as her opponents have supposed *a priori.* The action, from on high, which touched her at first in a more exterior and physical manner, she immediately internalized. The hesitations and brief resistance show the freedom of her growth. The messages guided her to a personal contact which became more and more perfect each year in a normal progressive way. She knows to Whom she is listening. She speaks to the Lord freely with love and an ever-growing friendship that moves towards intimacy and even indivisible union. In the first period, when she experienced this profound unity with the Lord, she said to Him with tender humor while having her ticket checked:

—When I think that we two are traveling on one ticket!

The Experts Reject the Hypothesis of Automatic Writing

Father Curty, an experienced exorcist of Cardinal Coffy of the Archdiocese of Marseilles, has rejected these trumped up charges.

They come from well-meaning people who know about channeling and automatic writing only from what they have read. This phenomenon, which is often discussed in a superficial way, is quite well-known by Father Curty in his capacity as an exorcist. He gives a clinical description of it in these terms:

The hand of someone who has given himself over freely to this sort of guidance writes by itself and does not write by conscious thought or intelligence. Instead, it moves by an unknown force which is not subject to the will of the writer. Sometimes, in extreme cases, it is the instrument all by itself (a pen or pencil), which, by the mere contact of a finger, begins to write a message.

Vassula's case is quite different. As we have said, the one whom she identifies as her guardian angel at first acted by a movement that was communicated to her; however, her own spirit always had a role in this. Since this involved a personal contact, she learned to listen to the voice of Christ. All of this occurred, according to the circumstances, in a very free and varied fashion and in complete gratuity. She wrote down what she heard. Today most often this happens without this moving of her hand. Father Curty has listed a description of these variations:

1. Vassula receives a locution or interior word from the Lord, but she is only able to write it down

when she gets home. As she recalls it, her hand is guided by the Lord.

2. Sometimes there is a dictation that she writes down as if she were a secretary or a typist, though she maintains her personal autonomy and her perfect contact with her surroundings. She can interrupt this dictation at any moment to answer the telephone and she can take it up again where she left off. Also, in this case, her personal writing is transformed into a "vertical, upright handwriting, always peaceful and measured in its respiration." Although the style of writing changes, Vassula still keeps full control of herself.

3. Sometimes Vassula receives just an infused interior light that is not expressed in words. It is what the mystics call a spiritual motion or an intellectual motion of the spirit. Vassula then interprets and expresses this intuited message. She takes her pencil to begin in her own normal handwriting, but instead she produces the beautiful hieratic handwriting, "as if to give this revelation a seal from on high." Father Curty concludes: "It is thus in no way automatic writing."

4. Finally, as if to convince us, the Lord at times proceeds in another way. When the messages are very long and the available time is too short, the Lord allows Vassula to write down the dictation in her own handwriting which is lively and alert. She is in no way influenced by this way of writing nor guided by some spirit. "Her spiritual experience then has nothing at all in common with auto-

matic writing. It is hieratic writing." It is, in other words, sacred and inspired.

The examples given by Father Curty do not exhaust the variety of situations that occur. I have personally examined this matter with Vassula, and there are still more varieties:

5. Sometimes she receives a message when she is at a typewriter, and she types the message that is in printed form. The means of transmission is of little importance.

6. Sometimes Vassula is speaking with other people, and, during the conversation itself, the Lord has her say His message orally without her voice taking on any unusual tone.

In a few words, the message that she receives in this intimate and personal way can be transmitted in various ways through a variety of means of expression and writing. It can be a material dictation with little reflection or it can involve an attentive hearing. It can be written down in the hieratic writing, or in her personal style, or even with a typewriter. It can be an intuition or "inspiration" without words or a rough sketch of an expression that requires an interpretation or explanation. In the case of the much-discussed phrase that was badly translated from English: "the Father and I are One," she hesitated to write the more subtle continuation under the form: "We are the same," or "We are oneness." The two expressions were correct in English because they are neuter. But the French (masculine) translation: "*nous sommes le même*" (in Italian "*lo stesso*") betrays the message.

However, the most important thing for making the distinction between automatic writing and Vassula's handwriting is that she receives these messages in love, that love which is so luminously personalized, devout and dedicated, gives these messages their attraction and makes so many superficial Christians grasp the beauty, the intimacy, and the transcendence of the Lord. This evangelical gratuity places us a thousand miles away from the confused experiences and the automatism of channeling. All the discussion on channeling has only added to the confusion. We should be serious and objective when we are engaged in discerning spiritual things. Father Curty has well expressed his discernment in saying that these inspired messages of Vassula are "a letter of Our Lord to His Church."

The Language of Love

A recent critic, whose text I have before my eyes, accuses her of being excommunicated as a divorcée, and so her communions are sacrilegious (a note published in *Il Sabato*).

In fact, her marriage with Mr. Per Ryden was celebrated according to the law of her Orthodox Church in Lausanne. This took place after an official regularization due to the failure of the previous marriage in which she had suffered a lot. Those who have the task of advising or judging in these matters (as in my own case) keep these personal matters in the area of priestly discretion without divulging the reasons. Her case presented no problems, and the ceremony of the bridal crowning was performed with all its liturgical value.

(The crowning is omitted in regularizations that have a penitential aspect.)

Let us not be too quick to accuse the Orthodox Church of laxity in this matter as did an opponent who, no doubt, is not very open to ecumenism. Each year in the USA there are more than 40,000 broken marriages that are annulled by the Catholic Church with an authorization for a new marriage. I know a number of fervent Americans (including seers) who are among them. Is it necessary to be stricter than the Catholic Church in these matters at a time when each church tries to resolve the problems posed by the plague of divorces as best it can according to different but convergent principles?

The Orthodox Church does it according to the "law of economy". They allow a humane solution tosituations which have become impossible for faith and morals. In the Orthodox Church the second marriage of the innocent party is celebrated without pomp and without the bridal crown. It has a penitential character (something that is not even dreamed-of in the Catholic Church).

The Catholic Church acts according to very strict principles of law. In this context American canon lawyers are hard at work. When a marriage has broken down to the point that it is psychologically irreversible, they ask if it is not perhaps due to some original defect or lack of consent. Some canon lawyers have drawn conclusions with solid reasons. The most serious of these is that a number of marriages that we celebrate are not valid due to the lack of the full consent that is demanded by the Church.

Formal Heresy?

The inquisitor is ready to give to any event and any vague rumor the worst possible interpretation. Behind the slightest ambiguity he sees an agglomeration of heresies. One of them wrote recently:

—"There is, in Vassula, at least one formal heresy about the soul. According to Vassula, the soul, before being infused in the body and contracting original sin, already saw God. That is a heresy. Jesus himself said that no one has ever seen God. The pre-existence of souls before their infusion in the body has been formally condemned by the Council of Constantinople" (543).

Let us move on beyond the date and the reference to the Council of Constantinople which has no connection with any objective reality, and let us also skip over the objections that we have already examined. Instead let us focus on the argument that is taken from the Gospel. It is true that John the Evangelist says in his prologue (1:18): "No one has ever seen God," and in 6:46, "No one has seen the Father."

But in the same Gospel Jesus also says:

—"He who sees me sees him who has sent me" (Jn. 12:45).

—"Whoever has seen me has seen the Father. Then how is it that you say 'show us the Father'" (Jn. 14:9 preceded by 14:7: "If you knew me, you would also know my Father.")

According to these words, also in this case one sees God. It would therefore be Jesus himself who is guilty of heresy according to the verdict of the inquisitor. In fact, there are lots of ways to see God, and the Gospel speaks of his transcendence that goes far beyond us to show how he has revealed himself. These texts, therefore, should be seen in the whole context and not in an isolated one to then be used as arms in a war against Vassula or other sincere Christians.

What she is talking about is not the beatific vision by a soul before its union with the body but the imprint of the Creator at the moment of the creation and immediate infusion of the soul in the body.

Failed Conversion?

Many adversaries say:

If it really were Christ who is appearing to Vassula, the first thing he would have said is: "Become a Catholic." If he did not say that, then it is not really Christ. It is the devil who keeps her in schism.

This is a very simplistic conclusion. There are Christians who have discovered the full authenticity of Catholicism but think for a long time to decide if they should change religions or if they should remain in their own church to work for ecumenical rapprochement. There are Catholics who roughly criticized Max Thurian for becoming a Catholic after a long period of thought and after having exercised responsibility within the inner core of the World Council of Churches. They accused him of "ecumenical insensitivity." Protestants were the most open and understanding about his decision of conscience which was bound to his deep faith in the Eucharist. Could it be that Catholics are more influenced by the Inquisition?

There is a precise reason for Vassula's position. She has an ecumenical mission. She has a prophetic vocation for a reunion starting from the place where she was born and baptized. She makes good use of ecumenical hospitality and, as we have already said, she is attacked from both sides:

- The Catholic side because she is Orthodox.

- The Orthodox side because she is too Catholic (as regards the pope, the Sacred Heart, the rosary and so forth.)

In place of her now-abandoned splendid social life, the Lord is creating within her an integral faith which is in no way syncretism. She broadly takes on the values of the three denominations in which she has been engaged throughout her life, which was at first less than fervent: Orthodoxy by her birth and baptism; Protestantism on the occasion of her two successive marriages; and Catholicism, thanks to the priests that she met to guide her in this unusual religious awakening.

When one knows even a little about her inner life and her loyal and transparent adventure, which is authentically Christian with no confusion; when one sees her life of direct contact with the Lord and her sensitive and informed openness to the entire Apostolic Tradition, then he can only feel pity for the temptation that has overcome Catholics who are in every other way worthy of esteem. How is it possible that their quarrel, at times echoed in respectable media, could present Vassula in such a twisted, deceptive way and in so little accord with their openness and their high spiritual level?

Let no one throw the first stone. Discernment is not easy. It is a place where temptation can be subtle. Let us draw the true lesson from this and not allow ourselves to be tricked by the *diabolos,* a master in the art of dividing and wounding Christians in their vital forces. If the messages of this or that seer say nothing to us, let them be. Nothing obliges you to accept them. But do not judge them too hastily without having seen the fruits that they produce. For Vassula, they are continually confirmed: conversions and healing.

A Heretical Translation

Another objection has been raised which has a valid point. In the Italian and French editions of the messages, Jesus says on several occasions: The Father and I are One and the Same: *Le Père et Moi nous sommes Un et le Même* (February 15, 1989; March 29, 1989; July 26, 1989; and in reference to the Holy Spirit, on October 11, 1988).

In French, as in Italian, the words "the same (*le même, lo stesso*)" are masculine and would seem to indicate that the Father and the Son are one and the same person. That would objectively be a heresy. In fact, they are a single Being, a single Essence, a single ontological Existence, but in three Persons who share in a common, identical communion.

There is no error in the original English text as it is written by Vassula's hand: "We are One and the Same."

In English, the word "same" is neuter and thus signifies a unity of being that is shared by the three Persons. In hearing this, Vassula understood, "The same, oneness," in other words, "unity" (or as English dictionaries say, "that which is numerically one").

The distinction of Persons is therefore in no way unclear in the messages received and transcribed by Vassula.

The Italian and French versions had translated the word as masculine due to the fact that the neuter does not exist in these languages. It will be necessary to change the translation as is being done in these editions right now.

Some people might object:

How is it possible that the readers of Vassula did not rise up in indignation in reading these heretical translations?

It is not that simple, for the translations are ambiguous rather than heretical. Most of the readers that I have spoken with about this matter had themselves interpreted and cleared up any ambiguities in light of the context. In the context, Vassula is always quite clear regarding the distinction of Persons with whom she is in distinctly different personal relationships. The readers had, themselves, understood the word Le Même in a neutral sense from the fact that the masculine at times has a neutral sense in French as in the comical grammatical saying, "*L'homme embrasse la femme*" (The man embraces the woman.) In other words, the words "man embraces" here means, includes, and refers to the two sexes in a general way (i.e. Mankind includes women).

The ambiguity of which we were speaking is so unlikely that the French Jerusalem Bible and the Osty Bible both translate John 19:30 with the masculine, which Vassula quotes as "My Father and I are One."

A careless reader might run the risk of understanding it to mean a sole person. However, the many reviewers of the Jerusalem Bible and millions of readers automatically gave the word "one" a neutral meaning which indicates a unity of being. Moreover, no one objected to this frequently read translation. Here again the context is enough to eliminate any heretical interpretation.

It is not easy to speak of the Trinity.

The most popular Italian translation of the Bible (which from now on will be used for the translations of Vassula) avoids translating John 10:30 with the expression, *Siamo uno* (We are One). It says, *"siamo una sola cosa."*—We are one thing. In this way it avoids any ambiguity, but at the price of a new disadvantage, for the Father and Son are not a thing. God is not an object.

Should we use the word "substance"? Although theologians and some Councils used this word, it is not the most happy choice either for sub-stance literally means "the deeper being beneath appearances," for example the substance of Christ is given under the appearances of bread and wine. But in God there is no deeper reality contrasted with a transitory one. There is no substance in contradistinction to the transitory.

What then are we to say if we wish to talk about these things either in the Bible or the messages of Vassula? A single essence (*Ousia* in Greek) would be the best translation but in French this makes people think of *essence* (gasoline). One might say: a sole Being or even a sole Existence. However, the word existence could suggest a psychological existence and obscure the distinct "I" which corresponds to each Person in their common divine existence.

It was important to dot our i's and cross our t's to show just how difficult it is to speak correctly of God, who is ineffable and lies beyond human speech in virtue of his transcendence. The words should certainly be precise, but they are always inadequate. A theological text can only be read well in the light of God.

It is therefore, in this light and in charity rather than in witch hunts and cutting down our neighbor that we have to take into consideration the inherent weaknesses in all human interpretations. If the Italian and French editions as well as the translations of John 10:30 are ambiguous and could be opportunely clarified or corrected, they are not formally heretical and it is for this reason that the accusation is inaccurate and extremist, even if we must thank the careful theologian who took note of this unfortunate ambiguity and gave the four correct references (except for a mistaken date of July 27, 1989 rather than July 26).

P.S. I thought I had come to the end of these misleading charges. Then in January again there were new ones from America. This time they were unleashed most notably in *The Wanderer* (which is often of a higher caliber). This attack appeared after a prayer meeting in which Vassula had been welcomed into the cathedral at Sacramento, California, by the bishop himself, Bishop

F. A. Quinn. He concelebrated the Mass and another Bishop [Donald Montrose] gave the sermon.

The fictional account of the meeting quite erroneously accused Vassula of wanting to have Church unity under the leadership of the World Council of Churches in Geneva.

In fact, Vassula has had a number of talks with the directors of it in December 1991 and January 1992.

She gave them the messages she had received for the unification of the date of Easter and for the unity of Christians through the co-operation of all. However, in no part in any of these messages did she ask for unity under the leadership of the World Council, which moreover, has no such pretension since it is a center for dialogue and for gatherings working toward unity.

On the other hand, quite often she has referred to Peter's successor, the foundation of unity willed by Christ (Mk. 16:16), who is today John Paul II , for example: "For the sheep that are not under the guidance of Peter, so that they return to Peter and be reconciled…So that there will be one flock and one Shepherd." Some Orthodox criticize her precisely for this "papism".

Clearly the inquisitors of 1993 are less conscientious than those of the Middle Ages who also had a systematic spirit but at least took the time to carefully interrogate their victims before these were led to the stake or having them executed by the civil authorities.

But no more parable. I would like, above all, that Vassula's detractors, men whom I esteem and with whom I generally share Catholic convictions, reflect on a problem of the church that has its importance. Hundreds of persons are converted by reading or listening to Vassula. These are serious, lasting, balanced conversions. I know many of them. For some respectable Christian theologians to disqualify that which has converted them can only trouble them. Certain ones ask themselves:

If for once Christianity convinces me, the theologians say "it's false, it's heretical, it's despicable, isn't it that Christianity [itself] is illusory?"

Moreover, the obstacles put in the way of Vassula's tours paralyze her fruitful evangelization. Have we nothing better to do and, if we are combative, at the hour when so many disastrous errors undermine the Church, why mobilize so many live forces against Vassula and Medjugorje where the work of God is so manifest?

Medjugorje, immense source of conversions, calls out the desperate eagerness of numerous impassioned detractors, certain ones who have authority. Msgr. Zanic furthermore said, on the very day when I'm writing this, on a French television network with a wide viewing audience:

"Medjugorje, it's only a move to make money and a lie of the Franciscans. Unfortunately they will never admit it, except in eternity."

These disconcerting attacks neutralize a great spiritual movement. The plan of the Peace of Our Lady has suffered from it. The Church has suffered from it.

The strangest thing is that certain supporters of Medjugorje are opposed to Vassula for the purity of Medjugorje, when Vassula is 100% for Medjugorje. She fights no one, she who is so fought against. Her only weapon is the love of Jesus. May the divine love between Christians and vigilance against the prince of darkness, genial artisan of the divisions tearing apart the Catholic Church, cause us to rediscover tolerance and understanding between sincere Christians. Our primary urgency is to fight against our divisions.

Inquisition Against Vassula

I had finished the French edition of this book to do the Italian edition, and, six months later, it is still necessary to lengthen the American edition. Because in a world where so many forces are unleashed to destroy a Church, where so many Christians fight between themselves and criticize the Pope, a large band of serious, fervent Christians have unleashed themselves against Vassula.

It is a true tidal wave in the Catholic press of the American USA. One asks oneself: What virus occasionally impels these great liberal people, champion of the rights of man that America is, to unleash itself against a person in the public eye, without measure and without reason? How have they successively assassinated the two Kennedy brothers? How have they so easily allowed the second after the first? How, after having made of John a great national hero and having raised up to him so many statues, museums, foundations, has his widow, one moment totally consecrated to his glory, returned him to the sewers?

"Here, to destroy people is considered a sport," said Vincent Foster, counselor to President Clinton, before the suicide to which this environment drove him.

Nixon had a pirate side [to his personality], but the dimensions of a true man of State. He was capable of stopping the inextricable Vietnam War and to tie the knot with China where the USA was then the hated number one enemy, and he had to leave in shame without power to accomplish his program.

I will not compare Vassula either to Kennedy or to Nixon, because she does not have their faults nor their weaknesses. Since the Lord has claimed her she is completely given to Him and to humanity, in peace and acceptance of all the suffering (stigmas included) without any rancor for the enemies eager to destroy her, without being acquainted with her out-of-the-ordinary spiritual adventure (and they don't want to be acquainted with it). Catholic writers and journalists, coming from a narrow, aggressive conservatism, only know how to invent her in order to caricature her, to defame and condemn her on all grounds: doctrine, religion, morals, her marriage, and even money. Her disinterest is absolute. She has given up her rights as an author, which could have made her a legitimate fortune. From those who invite her, she accepts only an airline ticket for herself and the priests who often accompany her to defend her vulnerability as a woman and an Orthodox, (both reasons for so much controversy).

The caricature unleashes itself to drive in the nail. They produce Vassula's effigy on the face of the green bill (a woman of money, to be sure)!; in place of the emblematic national figures, and, at the side, in place of the bank guarantee, the handwritten inscription: "Laurentin guarantees authenticity." There I am as a counterfeiter! That is how they kill reputations. "The tongue is a sword," said the Apostle James. Caricature, too.

Some American friends, anti-Vassula (whose personal opinion I respect) showed me this perverse caricature with a guileless smile, as if it were normal and well meaning, to turn me from my errors; by this time where the controversialists are priding themselves, this time Laurentin lacked discernment.

Others, (pro-Vassula) Tell Me:

Concerning the matter of reputation, one ought not let that pass by. One ought to apply the law of retaliation: "an eye for an eye, and a tooth for a tooth."

That is true if one wants to succeed in life, even in the Church, but the law of the Gospel is other than that and I have no intention of changing it. I will continue to defend Vassula in so much as she keeps to her exemplary line, as I defended Medjugorje and other serious clairvoyants to the detriment of my reputation. Because each time the Inquisitors proclaim: Laurentin no longer has any discernment, "He closes his eyes to heresies" (sic).

For the same reason, I'm responding here to the objections, without citing the names of the critics. Certain readers will regret it, but Christian charity and objectivity will win out in this regard. Some people I love and respect have been driven to such astonishing errors that it would be cruel to personalize. Controversy damages. The best show themselves here under their worst days and I would not like to treat them as if those spy reporters who photograph not the face but the backside of their victim, in some humiliating exercise of his existence.

I am writing solely for the defense of truth and the elementary human rights of man and woman and of the Christian. It grieves me to do it in opposition to sincere, respected people who are ordinarily more sensible. I have spoken with several of them and had to listen for some time before being able to speak a little in my own turn...and to pray with them. I had the feeling that they were closed-minded in their opposition, and I am more grieved by this dialogue of "deaf" persons than for all the rest. On the issues of theology, spirituality and current problems of the Church our agreement is deep and harmonious.

To one of these adversaries whom I invited to dinner for an exchange, which was fraternal, on our common bases, I said in conclusion:

Fundamentally, to destroy Vassula you were obliged to destroy Laurentin?

He did not deny it and justified himself on confiding in me the courage that he needed to engage himself in this spiritual combat: against sects and all deviance: When I began this controversy, my colleagues said to me:

Watch yourself; to attack Laurentin is serious; that could be dangerous.

I proceeded further.

He was without remorse and in perfect sympathy with our exchange; he didn't deem it wise to make the least excuse.

If it's spiritual warfare that inspires these controversies, the motive is assuredly estimable, but one wonders why it is Vassula whom they attack. Isn't it mistaking the target at the hour when so many serious errors would justify a fight?

"There is going to be a schism in America, if there aren't already schisms underground," an American friend told me on my last trip.

He called to mind not only pastoral homosexual allowances which have filled too many seminaries, but deviant theologies (reductionist exegesis), radical feminism that reforms Christianity by resorting to the use of non-Christian sources (goddesses of mythology, witchcraft, and lesbianism) as revealers of proper values to women. Doctrinal drifting of certain universities propagate themselves among the catechists to whom they give diplomas on forming and deforming their faith. Why is one so discreet on all the real dangers and why does one develop a good conscience while denouncing with mediatory scandal a woman totally given to Christ, who wholly accepts Catholic doctrine and whose word brings about profound, lasting conversions at all levels?

One deals gently with the most dangerous saboteurs of the truth whose power is feared, and one blames this woman, foreign and without defense, to whom the Holy Spirit has, however, given the grace to lead more hearts to God than most priests, myself included. What a waste of Christian energy that could have been better applied.

The controversies that, alas, multiply in the Church of today, carry a signature: dia-bolos, because the Greek name of the devil means "one who divides." He unleashes all his forces to put discord in the healthiest part of the Church. He targets to this end the best Christians, at a serious moment in the history of Salvation, at the threshold of events that hell dreads.

The Church of America is, however, exemplary for its openness to ecumenical dialogue. No false notes for the sake of courtesy. If there is a risk, it is more likely by an excess of openness, where Catholics become Protestant among the Protestants, on the points that divide us objectively.

I offer two examples of this (among others, at the highest level).

A celebrated American exegete has acquired a title of glory by writing books which cast doubt on the virginity of Mary. Between arguments for and against its historicity, the balance was equal, he expanded.

He accepted, without doubt, the virginity in the name of Catholic dogma, but accorded it no value in the realm of history. There were those who praised this liberalism that appeared to facilitate reconciliation on a minimum basis. He caused doubt to spread among Catholics on Mary's virginity in order to draw closer to other Christians on the lowest, most relative level of truth.

More recently, the presidential address of the last assembly of American Catholic exegetes upholds, with a science as seemingly erudite as it is unilateral and trendy, that the brothers of Jesus mentioned in the gospel were biological brothers, historically speaking: sons of Mary. The virginity, after the birth of Jesus, was, he recalls, a dogma to which Catholics ought to cling, but not belaboring its historicity opened the way to a greater ecumenical understanding.

Since ecumenism is most welcome for separated brothers so ready to understand each other to the point of damaging the dogma for reconciliation at the most basic levels, why does the American Catholic press unleash itself unilaterally against an Orthodox (the confession [of faith] closest to Catholicism), and an Orthodox who shares fully the faith and Catholic devotion, including the Pope, the Sacred Heart, and the Rosary? Her whole faith is an exceptional opportunity for ecumenism at the zenith to which Christ invites it to be.

Then why this burning to make of her a heretic? Why do our theologians of today, so concerned about the rights of man, take on the ardor of the judges of the Inquisition, who burned not only witches and Savanarola, but also Saint Joan of Arc? Certain of them reproach Vassula for profiting from the eucharistic hospitality open to Orthodox since the Council of Vatican II. More rigorous than the Council, they want excommunication for her in the etymological sense of the word. Why this hard-line approach, a stranger to our style today?

Vassula truly has no chance. While the Catholics are attacking her because she is Orthodox, and thus a heretic, her faith has earned her severe Orthodox attacks since her first tours in Greece because she is too wholly

Catholic. She has thus submitted herself to grave threats and intimidation. However, she has courageously returned there, and dialogues are open to her. She accepts them with perfect courtesy and ecumenical clarity. Could this then not serve as a lesson to Catholics who accuse her without dialoguing with her, as the Gospel invites us to do: "If your brother has anything against you, go first to be reconciled with your brother." No, the attitude of the controversialists is other than that. Vassula, being a woman and Orthodox, is not a sister. She is an enemy. She is the devil. Vitanda! One must avoid her, not speak to her, destroy her by surprise. Profit from the press to make her a case of contumacy, without advocate or defender.

All the forces of faith, of tradition, of morals, of spirituality, of the mystic ought to be understood, not to attack, but to sustain this converging prophetic force that the Holy Spirit has raised up to promote a new ecumenism founded on the most dynamic, most profound base: love.

This preamble was necessary to determine what answers to make to the new arguments issued by American controversialists these past months.

The Principal Objections

Two Slanders

1. Many keep going over the following accusation (like children who share chewing gum from mouth to mouth).

"At Sacramento she said: Jesus desires the unity of all Christians under the World Council of Churches," someone accuses.

Vassula never said that. She talked with the Ecumenical Council, furthermore as the last popes did, but her messages clearly and constantly say that unity must be achieved around the successor of Peter;

2. "Vassula predicted an earthquake in California and it didn't happen," says another.

A useless objection:

a. Vassula never predicted an earthquake in California.

b. There are frequent earth tremors in this fragile region of the West Coast. One wouldn't even have been able to blame her if she had predicted it.

The most serious controversialists grapple with doctrine to conclude with this unassailable slogan:

"These messages cannot come from Jesus Christ because they propagate false doctrine about Jesus Christ." The controversialist reproaches Vassula for incoherence where Jesus says to her:

"Let me edit what I wrote." NB9:7

Very simply, Jesus had dictated a message to her that she had written unexpectedly. After that, he asked her to copy (edit) in the notebook.

This criticism seems to ignore the intimate collaboration where Vassula never ceases to be guided by Christ: to listen, to write, and, for publication, to discriminate between private messages, which are personal to her, and public messages, alone destined for publishing. When Vassula recopies, with publication in mind, her hand is again moved from above and resumes hieratic writing. Finally, Jesus sometimes adds a development or refinement to the final edition.

To Fear or Not to Fear?

The critic reproaches her also for this invitation of Christ: "Never fear me": this contradicts the Bible that frequently calls us to fear God, he objects. The critic is doubly at fault.

1. The Bible says frequently, from Old Testament times to the annunciations to Zachariah and to Mary: "Fear not."

2. Moreover, following the text of Vassula on June 4, 1987, Christ finishes by saying: *"Never fear Me... fear Me only if you rebel against Me."* NB12:61. He said it even more strongly on May 27, 1987: *"If you rebel against Me, I will treat you as a Judge"* [would treat you]. NB12:31.

Trinitarian Errors?

The most serious attacks concern the Trinity. On reading them, I was impressed. Could I have badly read Vassula, I asked myself? The ambiguities that exist in all prophetic, poetic, or mystical texts, even biblical, would they be demeaned by assumed errors? I lost much time trying to find incriminating phrases. They appeared entirely different in their context, stripped of the distortions and the changed nature to which the passion of the heresy seekers had submitted them.

Patripassianism

The most reputed theologian among Vassula's adversaries thought he had found in her the ancient heresy called "patripassianisme" of Noet, Epigone, Cleomene and Praxas, for whom the Father is himself incarnated and suffered the Passion, because to them, he only had one person, no Trinity.

In the original manuscript, of which the edition has erased the references to render more difficult control over the accusations, the author gives four references to the original English text according to the first (anastasique)? Edition. NB10:18+[1]; NB18:10+; NB54:29+; NB48:38+.

1. On April 7, 1987, it is not the Father who is speaking, which is, moreover, very rare for Vassula. It is Jesus, as she and her readers have always recognized him and as the context indicates. NB10:18

That which has led the author to confusion is that sometimes Vassula calls Jesus "Father," according to a title given to the King Messiah by Isaiah 9:10. And if he is our brother as a man, he is Father as God, Author of his own existence. Thus he calls his disciples, "My little

---

1. In his dactylographic text, Vassula's adversary always cites the 1st English edition: the offset reproduction of the manuscript (not the second, nor the typographical).

children" (John 13:33). Vassula saw this filial relationship at the same time as being brotherly and spousal. These diverse facets are very well articulated for this married woman, who does not confuse the human plan with the mystical. Happily, because if she used the language of the Song of Songs: "Let him not kiss thee with the kisses of his mouth" (Sg:1:3), or even of certain mystics, celebrating their spousal marriage with Jesus, she would receive a terrible avalanche of criticism. By the simple fact that she uses the verb "to feel" to signify the love she owes Christ or that Christ has for us, her fault-finder accuses her of sentimentalism and eroticism quite displaced in its sexual overtones. However, Vassula is without ambiguity. If Jesus kisses her, it is on the forehead, like a father. Everything is as it should be, in the realm of opinion as in the realm of theology. Christianity has never endowed with guilt, neither the heart nor opinion.

2. In the second incriminating passage:

November 8, 1987, the heavenly interlocutor says: *"My Cross is on you, bear It with love. My Cross is the door to true life, embrace It willingly. Abnegation and suffering lead into a divine path."* NB18:10

It is Jesus who speaks, and it is clear, since he says in the first Me: *"Me, (Moi) your Jesus."* Then why attribute it to the Father, why lance Vassula with the poison arrow of Patripassianism?

3. In the third incriminating passage it is Jesus who speaks of his cross and the context is most clear. It is Jesus alone who speaks on that particular day, for the duration of several pages. NB54:15+

That which has permitted the inquisitor to find the heresy that he is looking for, is that in the preceding lines, where Jesus echoes Jn 12:23–25, he calls to mind the moment where he announced the imminent arrival of his "hour" (Jn 12:23), and where the voice of the Father had just glorified him (12:24–25). But it is He who calls forth from the passage the voice of the Father, and not the Father who speaks in all the pages.

4. The accuser believed he had found the erroneous attribution of the Passion to the Father in a fourth passage. In fact, in this passage, Vassula hears successively the voice of the Father, who alone says: "*My child*"; then that of the Son: "*penetrate my wounds, eat my Body and drink my Blood...*" NB48:38

Quotation marks, asterisks and a manuscript note at the bottom of the page indicate the change of interlocutor:

"*Now, it is the Son who speaks,*" says the note.

The theologian, who read too quickly, attributes to the Father that which the Son says. He has, no doubt, the excuse of working on the handwritten text, worried about exactness. But after that he would have had to give attention to the least details to not distort the text.

Ambiguities Transformed into Errors

I cannot continue indefinitely. That would be as tedious for the reader as for me. In brief, the critic reproaches the Jesus of Vassula for saying:

"*I am Yahweh.*"

The accusation is less serious, because abstractly, Jesus could have said it, since he is God, the only God revealed by the Old Testament. But the name Yahweh, which the Jews do not pronounce, out of respect, designates God according to his transcendence, as "Source of the Trinity," so say the Fathers of the Church. It is thus of the Father that it is fitting to say, *"I am Yahweh,"* more than of the Son, by fact of these important nuances. But in all the incriminating passages, it is certainly the Father who is speaking. On March 20, 1991, he says: *"My Son."* NB50:42

On February 16, 1987, the Son starts to speak in the line introduced by the word later. NB7:61

On April 13, 1991, it is certainly the Father who is speaking, since he says a little later: *"My Son."* The accusation is thus faulty. NB51:1–7

The critic wonders, with all the more reason, that Christ says: *"I am the Trinity."* (NB23:42; NB34:63; NB35:8 NB38:27) It is more ambiguous. Enlightened by the context near and far; Christ is one of the Trinity. He possesses of it all being, without diminution. He identifies himself with the Trinity that is One. He speaks in his name from the fact that it is the unity of one God in three persons who assume it as part of the whole.

The Inquisitor did not specify that Vassula evokes here a Trinitarian vision, where she sees Jesus in three dimensions, as on those optical images where one sees three personages in a single one. She seems to allude to these representations of the Trinity, by Magdalith, where on a single and same design one reads, either a single face who is the Father, or two other well-articulated representations that make up the Son and the Spirit. It is easy to fall into the trap of symbolic language.

Vassula, careful of this ambiguity, justifies it most notably by precedents. Untiring reader of Symeon the Theologian, she sends me photocopies of Trinitarian texts with this observation by his editor, Basil Krivoscheine, who comments by saying:

At the mystical level, Symeon [sic] addresses himself sometimes to the Trinity as to a single Person. The divine essence converses with Symeon in the first person (in The Light of Christ, chapter 19, p. 290).

On July 25, 1989, e.g., he says *"Me, [Moi] the Holy Trinity, I am One and the Same."* Naturally in the sense where certain theologians transpose nature and Personne in psychological terms by saying:

One I and two Me(s) in Christ. NB34:63

One ME and three I (s) in the Trinity.

It is difficult to find an adequate accuracy in the expression of this Mystery: 3=1. It defies mathematics and language. One could not know how to be too vigilant.

A Falsification

Vassula had already made me see that it was necessary to correct here the French translation, where one read in the masculine Un et le même, that which would be inadmissible, with the masculine designating la Personne, but Une et la même: which demonstrates the unity of the Trinity. This error evidently doesn't exist in the English; the neuter character of One and the same is not an error but is ambiguous.

Vassula specifies elsewhere (November 23, 1987):

"The Son is in the Father. They are only one. The Holy Trinity is ONE and THE SAME: three Persons but a single God: one and three;" NB18:50

Along the same lines, October 10, 1989:

"Me (Moi), I, your Lord Jesus Christ, [am] heaving My sighs of Love upon your forehead and with Great Love I bless each one of you to unite you and be one as the Holy Trinity is One and the Same, you too be one under My Holy Name." NB37:46–47

In the line of Jesus' discourse at the Last Supper (Jn 17): "Be one as we are One." The messages to Vassula distinguish at each step the plurality of Persons in ontological and metaphysical unity, for God, in the unity of the body of Christ for us, according to the invitation of Jesus, "Be one as we are One."

The critic still incriminates a commentary of July 8, 1990, where Vassula totally confuses the Persons: the Father would be "himself the son and the Holy Spirit." N43:61

Actually, Vassula mentions the three persons successively that the ill-meaning critic is confusing:

> Jesus in this whole passage mentions:
> The Father,
> Himself, as the son,
> and the Holy Spirit,
> showing the action and the presence of the Holy Trinity.

The theologian critic has unfortunately eliminated the comma that separates the Father from the Son. Thus has he understood: Jesus mentions the Father <u>as being himself</u> the son and the Holy Spirit!

It is very serious to omit a comma. When I was a scholar, I was taught the importance of punctuation (which ought to be included also in the English translation); the accusation changes meaning according to how one punctuates:

The judge says: "the accused is a thief"

or

"The judge," says the accused, "is a thief."

In many cases, one slanders Vassula squarely by perceiving her to say things she never said. The theologian whose accusations I'm allowing myself to reexamine takes care to make up things. He has thoroughly examined the texts at length. In the ardor of his witch-hunt, he reads the texts from the outside, across a deforming prism, in searching for heresy that he sincerely and unconsciously invents, isolating the text from the context without paying sufficient attention to the indication of quotation marks, notes, and other indications that might prevent all confusion.

For Vassula, who has an intimate, profound dialogue with the Trinity, the distinction of the Persons is evident. She recognizes each between Them, right away, as we might identify the voice of our friends on the telephone, without them having any need of saying who it is. Thus has she not proved the need to multiply footnotes that might be useful for ill-meaning readers.

"My habitual readers are not deceived by all that," she said to me with a sorrowful surprise for the caricature of her messages propagated by the controversialists.

That is a totally erroneous interpretation of the text. On reproducing Vassula's footnote, he caused the comma to be omitted from the English text: a very important comma between The Father, and Himself that cleanly separates the Father and the Son there where the denouncer introduces confusion.

The Suffering of Christ

Another series of objections condemns the texts where Christ talks about suffering for our sins.

Christ no longer suffers and God does not suffer: yet another heresy! The controversialist slowly develops.

In brief, a number of mystics speak of the sufferings of Christ for sin, as if current, without anyone incriminating them for it. They and their commentators explain it by diverse methods, sometimes embarrassing. The best [methods] consider the coinciding of time and of eternity in the eternal Person of Christ. Because if his physical suffering is recorded in a past older than 19 centuries, each moment of his Passion (like his life) is synchronistic with his eternity that resembles all the moments of time. The eternal I of Christ is able to thus speak of his sufferings that always belong to the present of his eternity. Nothing is abolished by his earthly life. It is with this totality of his life, that he is present in the Eucharist. Thus are we able to rediscover there his birth at Christmas and his Resurrection at Easter. It is what Pascal meant by a concise phrase for which no one has ever reproached him:

"Jesus is in agony until the end of the world."

It is the manner most spoken of to explain the complaints that the suffering Christ addresses to our world of today.

If one wanted to use against the controversialist the same bad procedures that he uses against Vassula, one would become indignant on saying:

"For this theologian, God is indifferent to sin. It's all the same to him. He has played the comedy of suffering in order to incite us to pity. His divinity was sheltered. It didn't get wet. On thus dismissing suffering, the controversialist finally makes a parody of the Passion. He fails to recognize that it is, indeed, God in Person (the eternal I of the Son of God who suffers for us)."

This is evidently not what the controversialist means although his criticism suggests it. He well knows, I think, that God who is Love, that this Love is not a stranger to what we call feeling. The Bible accords him, rightly, "bowels of mercy" and it is thus that he gave the greatest proof of love: his suffering and his death for us whom he loves.

Indifference

Some say the ecumenism of Vassula would propagate indifference. The objections that are made to her join those that are made to the Virgin at Medjugorje. I have responded specifically and at length to these in the book on the <u>Messages of Mary at Medjugorje Chrono-logical Corpus,</u> (p. 344–349). The ambiguities and the answers are parallel. When the Christ of Vassula says: "All Churches are mine," he affirms his power and his authority as Creator. Everything belongs to God. More-over, his mercy is open to all people of good will, beginning with sinners, without forgetting heretics who are victims of their own mistakes. That is what the texts of Vassula mean and nothing other. Furthermore, she speaks of the Body of Christ less as a mystical Body (the visible Church and its invisible extensions in those who are faithful to the Holy Spirit) than as the gathering of creatures for whom Christ is the "Firstborn" (Eph 1:15) according to Saint Paul, in the way that he is "the head of all principalities, of all powers," that is to say, of the angels (Eph: 2:15).

Vassula is a stranger to indifference and to relativism. When one accuses of heresy this Jesus by whom she transcribes the messages (sometimes not without cau-tion nor hesitation on the words and the course of events), she suffers from it and she remains scrupu-lously attentive to correct distortions or inaccuracies in certain translations. Indifference and relativism are generally frequent with "modern" theologians, al-though not with Vassula. She gives careful attention to exterior guidelines which she has been studying for a short time. Her exactness comes from her experience, even of God and his light, often superior to that of the theologian that I am. That gives her a well-informed sense of faith and in our painful dialogues on this useless controversy, I have never been able to trip her up. Nothing is easier than having a theological conversation with her, and it is a shame that her critics have avoided it. If they had entered into a fraternal dialogue with her before crushing her with their large mallet, they would have ascertained her light and her subtlety favorable to a profitable exchange, even for a well-informed theologian. I sense myself to be in a very humble position before many of the mystics I have met. If they don't dispose of the criteria and of the language that I have acquired at length from studying and teaching, they will penetrate interiorly more deeply the Mystery of God and his living relationship to people.

"I don't accept the messages of Vassula as coming from Christ because their doctrines on Jesus are false," say the critics.

For my part: I don't accept the criticism that this doctrine is false, by the fact that their critiques, which lead astray, falsify it as we have seen.

The clear texts of Vassula only speak of love. They flow from the source. Why must they be dismembered, torn to pieces, distorted from the outside? As the heretics were able to pull their heresies from the Bible, the controversialists pull from prophetic texts received by Vassula heresies that are totally foreign to her. They are the doing of the inquisitors and not of her messages.

The law of Christian reading is sympathy: that it concerns the Bible, the prophets, saints and Doctors of the Church and even brothers of good will, [even] be they separated brothers. Only a benevolent reading grasps each text in the light in which it was written, and interprets it according to the convergence of the context, in place of transforming the inevitable ambiguities in errors meriting excommunication or burning at the stake, according to the epoch in which one lives.

Even a Savanarola, that Dominican whom some would like to canonize, was burned, following his prophetic critique of unworthy popes. Brother, Vassula doesn't want you to have slandered her. She suffers because the messages of the Lord are caricatured and misrepresented. She suffers because slander obliges her to renounce momentarily, for the good of peace, a mission that carries such fruit in your country. Under the spitting she remains mute and prayerful. Having thus also toward her the kindness that is fitting between Christians without there being the pain of making appeal to the rights of man, to the rights of woman, to the rights of her reputation that has been gravely wounded. Let's forget it and turn the page, once these illusions go away. I would like for each one to finish this book as I end it, with a prayer for her friends, and for her enemies as well, that enemies may cease to be such.

Personal Testimony
Vassula Ryden

Marian Conference
Sacramento, California

March 1993

Yahweh visited me,
like a gust of wind His Spirit lifted me
and showed me His Countenance;
He revealed to me:
Tenderness, Love and Infinite Goodness,
He then showered me with Blessings and offered
me Manna
in abundance to share It with my brothers;
He walked with me in the land of oblivion,
from down among the dead He took me,
among those who have forgotten Him He raised me,
restoring the memory of my soul.

O Lord, Yahweh, how grateful I am!
May Your Sweetness O Lord be on us all.
Blessed be Yahweh for ever and ever. Amen.

(NB 57:3–4) (1–16–92)

God Calls Us to Him
to Live Holy

For those who do not know this prophetic revelation, I tell them that, on the whole, it is a call of Mercy and Love from God. It is a call to repentance, reconciliation, peace and unity. God is calling us to return to Him, change our lives and live holy as He is Holy.

From the very beginning of my call, Jesus, with insistence, asked me to change my life and live holy. He asked me to allow Him to peel off me everything that attached me to the world. As I was not being cooperative with Jesus, at one stage He even challenged me and asked me:

"Are you really seeking me?"

Jesus made me understand, from the beginning, that we cannot live two lives. We cannot have two loves. We have to choose. We cannot be the dwelling place of the Holy Spirit and at the same time store up our passions within us where the Spirit is supposed to be. Jesus will not tolerate that we keep within us any passion, no matter how small that one could be. Many times He says in the messages: *"I do not want to meet within you any rival."*

In one message, God says that the secret of holiness is devotion to Him. God wants us to abandon this superficial way of living and devote ourselves to Him. He wants us to lead a Eucharistic life because, as He said: *"The Eucharist is the Life of the Church."*

The Apostasy and the Rebel
The Two Signs
Preceding the End of Times

In these messages, Our Lord asks us to be vigilant and recognize the signs of the end of times. Saint Paul wrote in II Th.2, that we should be able to recognize these times by two significant Signs.

The first Sign would be that of a general Apostasy, which means rejection of faith, rationalism, rebellion, egoism and the coldness of the hearts of men.

The second Sign would be that of the Rebel, the Antichrist. Jesus, today, describes the Antichrist as in the Johannine Epistles (I Jn. 2:18, 22; I Jn. 4:3; II Jn.7). It means antichrists in heresiarchs of today.

Daniel, the prophet, said of him in Chapter 11:31:

Forces of his will come and profane the sanctuary citadel; they will abolish the perpetual sacrifice and install the disastrous abomination there.

Christ explains to us that the Rebel today is a spirit. This spirit of rebellion is an abomination in the Eyes of God. It is the disastrous abomination of which the prophet, Daniel, spoke.

I shall take word after word to explain this very important passage of which Daniel, the Prophet, spoke because it is relevant. It is relating to the apostasy of today. Remember that Jesus Himself in Mt. 24:15 warned us of these times and of the disastrous abomination.

115

Each soul is the Holy place of God. We are God's temple; we are God's dwelling place; we are God's sanctuary citadel.

The perpetual sacrifice is the Holy Communion, Christ's Sacrifice.

The disastrous abomination is, as I said before, the spirit of rebellion.

The rebellious spirit installs itself within the soul just where the Holy Spirit ought to abide. This spirit then becomes an antichrist, for it denies the Divinity of Christ. It denies that Christ resurrected with His Body. The Holy Communion to it means nothing. It sees everything with its own light and rationalistic mind.

A person with this spirit of rebellion believes that he can be like God. He believes he knows good and evil. He repeats, therefore, the same error of Adam and Eve. His aim is to free himself from the Law of God, and become like God.

When the person with this rebellious spirit cuts his intimate union with God, he instantly dries up and is ready to be thrown on the fire to be burnt, for the soul becomes cold and arid. Thus if the Holy Spirit is rejected, Satan then will act freely in that soul.

Jesus told us in Jn. 15:6:

Anyone who does not remain in me is like a branch that has been thrown away—he withers; these branches are collected and thrown on the fire and they are burnt.

When a soul apostatizes it rejects the Holy Spirit from within it from Whom it could obtain its virtues to produce good fruit.

The Holy Spirit and the False Prophets

The Holy Spirit is like the Tree of Life planted in our inmost being which turns our soul into another Paradise. When this Tree of Life has taken root inside us, it changes our lives. When we have the Tree of Life planted in us, we can only produce good fruits, and these fruits are pleasing to God.

The Holy Spirit is already preparing us for the Kingdom of Heaven and it will surpass the Garden of Eden. If we reject the Holy Spirit, we will be rejecting the Kingdom of Heaven. We would instantly be erring as an outcast in the wilderness where death would be awaiting us.

The Holy Spirit again is like a River, saturating the soul with virtues.

God our Father tells us also in these messages that, in the last days, many false teachers and false prophets will arise. In the message of 13th December, 1992, He tells us:

I am reminding you to beware of the false teachers and the false prophets who induce in your soul desolation and misinterpret the gospels, telling you that the Holy Spirit is not with you to remind you of your foundations nor of where you come from. They have already made a desolation out of your soul and dug a vast gulf between you and Me, your Father. Do not let them expand this desolation in your soul and mislead you into believing I have left you orphans. These false prophets have made out of My Son, Jesus, a liar and out of the gospels an echoing cymbal, empty with emptiness. They made out of My Word a gaping grave; so beware of those false teachers, who tell you that My Holy Spirit cannot descend to perform in you miracles and wonders....beware of them who keep up the outward appearance of religion but reject the inner power of it, the inner power that is My Holy Spirit."—NB 63:63–64

It is clear that, in this passage, God wishes to warn us against those whom we call the modernists. The teachers and the prophets are some modern theologians who do not believe in miracles, nor in the resurrection of Christ. They do not believe, either, in the Real Presence of the Eucharist. They make their own law and explain the Scriptures with their rationalistic light and not with the Transcendent Light of the Holy Spirit.

At any rate, we see clearly how one cannot understand without the Light of the Holy Spirit. For example, when even good people attack me and, with rage, combat these messages, they extract words and sentences from their context and misinterpret the meaning. Naturally it would sound wrong. I am taking this opportunity to ask them to follow the sound advice of Pope Benedict XIV in the Constitution which he prefixed to the Index. The Pope says:

We give warning that it must be diligently remembered that a correct judgment of the true sense of an author cannot be arrived at unless the book be read all through, in all its parts, and the things found in different places be compared one with the other, and unless the whole scope and end of the author be attentively considered and examined. The author is not to be judged by one or other proposition torn from its context, or disjoined from other propositions to be found within the same book. For it frequently happens that what an author says carelessly or obscurely in one part of his work is explained clearly, fully and distinctly in another part; so that the darkness which seemed to conceal something wrong is afterwards altogether dissipated, and the proposition is seen to be free of all error.

Many times these people rationalize the mystical and ascetical language with arationalistic hermeneutic.

Jesus tells us that in the last days, many would have the outward appearance of religion, but would have rejected the inner power of His Church; this power which is His Holy Spirit.

On April 15, 1991, Jesus explains to us that this inner power of His Church is His Holy Spirit. He says:

"The inner power of My Church is My Holy Spirit in it, alive and active; like a heart in a body, My Holy Spirit is the Heart of My Body which is the Church.

The inner power of My Church is My Holy Spirit who gives freely and distributes its gifts and its graces, so that the Church gets some benefit.

The inner power of My Church is My Holy Spirit, the Reminder of My Word, revealing nothing new, but the same instructions given by the same Spirit.

The inner power of My Church is My Holy Spirit, that transfigures, uplifts and turns you into real copies of Myself.

The inner power of My Church is My Holy Spirit, this Fire which enlivens you, purifies you and makes out of your spirit columns of fire, ardent braziers of love, living torches of light, to proclaim without fear My Word, becoming witnesses of the Most High and teaching others to look only for Heavenly things.

The inner power of My Church is My Holy Spirit, the Life and the Breath that keeps you alive and makes your spirit desire Me, calling Me: Abba.

If you refuse, My child, and suppress the gifts of My Holy Spirit, what services will you be able to do and offer Me?

Do not be like corpses that keep up the outward appearance of religion but reject the inner power of it with futile speculations, thus limiting Me in My Divinity.—NB 51:15–18

But it is not only Jesus who teaches us again the Riches and the Treasures of His Holy Spirit, but also the Father. There are some passages which I can never forget when I was under His dictation. For instance, I cannot forget the tone of His Voice when Our Father in Heaven gave me those passages when His Holy Spirit covered with His shadow Our Blessed Mother. The joy of the Father was indescribable.

Here is an excerpt that was given to me on the 5th October, 1992, which will be in the sixth volume:

Today more than ever I am sending you My Holy Spirit to renew you, yet, for how long will this generation keep resisting My Holy Spirit?

Tell Me, can a body live without a heart? Learn that My Holy Spirit is the Heart of the Body which is the

Church. Learn that My Holy Spirit is the Breath of the Church, the Essence of zeal for Me your God.

My Holy Spirit is the sweet Manna of Heaven nourishing the poor. Happy the man who opens his heart to My Holy Spirit, he will be like a tree along a river, yielding new fruit every season.—NB 62:36–37

...My Holy Spirit is the zest of your life, the Royal Crown of Splendor, the Diadem of Beauty from My Mouth, the radiant Glory of the Living One, the Secret Revelation of your creation.

My Holy Spirit is the flavor of your homilies in My Assemblies...and the fulfillment of your Times.

He is the Flaming Fire of your heart and the perception of My Mysteries.

My Holy Spirit is the theme of your praises to Me revealing to your heart that I AM WHO I AM, revealing to your spirit that I am your Abba, and that you _are_ My offspring, My seed.—NB 62:41–42

I, the Creator of the heavens and earth, tell you My Holy Spirit is the Spouse of the Bride, of She who held the Infant Who was to save you and redeem you, and in Whom through His Blood you would gain freedom and forgiveness of your sins. He is the Spouse of the One Whom He found like a garden enclosed, holding the rarest essences of virtues, a sealed fountain, the loveliest of Women, bathed in purity because of Her unique perfection. My Spirit came upon Her and covered Her with His shadow and glorified Me making Her the Mother of God, the Mother of all humanity and the

Queen of Heaven; such is the Richness of My Holy Spirit.—NB 62:42–44

This was what I heard from the very Mouth of God regarding the activity of His Holy Spirit.

My Call

And now, I will go back to the time when Jesus revealed Himself to me in the beginning. He asked me this question:

"Which house is more important, your house or My House?" I answered:

"Your House."

He then told me: *"Revive and embellish My House. Unite My House."*

When He told me this, I panicked, for I knew very well that, in the condition He found me, it was an impossible thing He was asking of me. So I told Him that He should go and find someone else who could do what He desired. But He said:

"No. I want you. I want a nothing."

And in His message of 21st February, 1987, He specified:

"Do you love Me?" I answered: *"Very much, You know I do."* He said: *"Do you desire that others love Me too?"* I replied: *"Yes, this is my wish now."* Jesus said: *"Work then with Me, and write down all that I tell you."* I told Him then

that this was like a miracle to be guided by Him in this way. And He said:

I willed it. I have chosen you to show the world that I need neither authority nor holiness. I have chosen a mere child, helpless and sinful, with no authority and knowing no one in power, to manifest through this weak instrument with My Grace, My Peace and Love I have for you all. I want to convey to this dark world My Message, thus showing My effusions to the world, for My Mercy is ineffable, and My affection beyond any human understanding.... I come to proclaim My Message to you all and turn you away from your evil doings. My Word will be like a cedar, spreading out its branches like arms, healing your wickedness, feeding your misery, and delivering you from evil. I come once more to enlighten this dark world and revive this flickering flame about to extinguish and cover you with My Peace.—NB 8:17–20

Unity

Since the very beginning, Christ expressed His longing to unite the Churches. He desires that we become one. It is His priestly Prayer which is the most moving, and a supplication to the Father:

May they all be one. Father, may they be one in us, as you are in me and I am in you, SO THAT THE WORLD MAY BELIEVE IT WAS YOU WHO SENT ME....

SO THAT THE WORLD MAY BELIEVE IT WAS THE FATHER WHO SENT HIM, we have to become one, meaning to unite, so that all the world believes in Jesus Christ, the Son of God.

I have chosen a few excerpts from these ecumenical messages to read to you. The first one was given to me the 2nd June, 1987. Jesus had given me a vision which lasted most of the morning. I saw three iron bars, rigid but near each other. Then Jesus told me:

> *Unite those lines. To unite you must all bend; you must be all willing to bend by softening.... How could their heads meet, unless they all bend?*—NB 12:55–56

Here Christ is inviting us all to bend ourselves, in humility and in love, for later on in the message He says that the key to unity is love and humility. Further in His messages of unity, He enumerates the virtues that would lead us to unity.

Our Blessed Mother, on the 23rd September, 1991, tells us this:

> *Treason barricades unity among brothers, insincerity of heart induces God's Cup to augment. They wrenched the Body of My Son, divided It, mutilated It and paralyzed It. ...The Keys to Unity are Love and Humility...I implore My children to unite in their hearts and voices and rebuild My Son's primitive Church in their heart. I am saying My Son's primitive Church, since that Church was constructed on Love, Simplicity, Humility and Faith. I do not mean you to reconstruct a new edifice, I mean you to reconstruct an edifice <u>inside</u> your heart. I mean you to knock down the old bricks inside your heart,*

bricks of disunion, intolerance, unfaithfulness, unforgiveness, lack of love, and reconstruct My Son's Church by reconciling. You need intense poverty of the spirit and an overflow of wealth of generosity, and not until you understand that you will have to bend, will you be able to unite.—NB 54:44–47

Jesus is more severe for He reproaches those who are not sincere. On October 7, 1991, He gave this message: (this is just an excerpt)

Their division has separated My Heart from theirs...tell them that I want Peace and One Church under My Holy Name...Tell them also how I abhor insincere hearts; their solemnities and their discourses weary Me...I cannot congratulate a dying Church nearing putrefaction. Tell those who want to hear that: unless they lower their voices, they shall never hear Mine. Should they lower their voices then they will begin to hear Mine and thus do My Will.—NB 55:2–6

Jesus' Will is to unify the date of Easter. This is what He says:

Will I, brother, one more season go through the pain I have been going through year after year? Or will you give Me rest this time? Am I going to drink one more season the Cup of your division? Or will you rest My Body and unify, for My sake, the Feast of Easter?—NB 55:30–31

It is obvious from His words that Jesus' Body is in great Agony, and to this very day the One whom we crucified and recrucify daily, continues to pray to the Father that we may all be one:

O Father! Reconcile them and remind them that by My death on the Cross I have given them My Peace. Give them the Spirit of Truth in its fullness into their hearts and when they see their nakedness they will understand. Forgive them, Father, for they know not what they are doing.—NB 55:58–59

Our Holy Mother and the Alliance of the Two Hearts

Up to now I have spoken about the Apostasy, the Holy Spirit and the Unity.

I would have liked to show you, though, how Our Blessed Mother taught me gently and slowly and how She taught me that Her Heart is united with Our Lord's Heart.

One day I had asked Jesus where, in the Bible, Our Holy Mother is mentioned and He asked me to read Ap. 12, where it says:

As soon as the devil found himself thrown down to the earth, he sprang in pursuit of the woman, the mother of the male child, but she was given a huge pair of eagle's wings to fly away from the serpent into the desert, to the place, (which is Egypt,) where she was to be looked after for a year and twice a year and half a year.

The passage continues of how the devil went away to make war on the rest of her children, that is, us, who bear witness for Jesus.

Today the Two Hearts, like Two Witnesses, witness Their Love. Both manifest themselves to us to teach us again how to live holy. Here is an excerpt of a message I received on Christmas Eve, 1991:

Elijah and Moses have come already and you have not recognized them but treated them as you pleased; you have not listened to Our Two Hearts, the Immaculate Heart of My Mother and My Sacred Heart, you faithless generation...Our Two Hearts are anointed and are living. They are like a sharp sword, double-edged, prophesying, but the rebellious spirit in this generation is recrucifying My Word, the double-edged Sword, and is rejecting Our Two Hearts who speak to you today; just like Sodom's and Egypt's rejection of My Messengers. This era's stubbornness has surpassed Pharaoh's because their claims to their knowledge have become a battlefield to My Knowledge; indeed Our Two Hearts have become a plague to the people of the world.—NB 56:62–64*

By this Our Lord wants to show us that Their Two Hearts today, like two witnesses, witness Their Love together, but the world mocks Them. They do not listen to Them. Not only do they not listen to Them, but the world persecutes Them and blasphemes Them. The world treats Their Two Hearts as they please. (Read Ap. 11)

We find people who do not believe that Our Blessed Mother today manifests Herself everywhere in the world. There are some who even criticize Her, saying that She talks too much and repeats Herself. YES! She will continue to repeat Herself and She will continue to talk to us until She pierces through those thick layers of deafness.

Our Lord tells us in these messages that Our Lady is preparing and is smoothing the road of return for Him. As She was created to give us our Messiah, today She manifests Herself almost everywhere to prophesy to us and prepare us for the Second Pentecost. As a patient and loving mother educating her children, She, too, educates us to school us back into holiness. She wants Her children to be ready to receive Our Lord in His Glory.

Russia

Now I will have a few words on the prophetic messages on Russia because it is Russia that will glorify God the most.

Jesus tells us:

Soon the glory will be given to Me in its fullness and Russia will govern the rest of My children in holiness…I God designed Russia for My Glory and it is through her that light will shine out of her darkness, it is through her light that your generation's heart will be enlightened with the knowledge of My Glory; I shall pour out My Spirit on the House that I had given her and I will display My Holiness in her to honor My Name…I will lift her to become the head of many nations; in her poverty I will rebuild My Kingdom.—NB 63:18–20

So far I have received eighteen prophecies concerning Russia.

Jesus Thirsts for Lack of Love

Jesus is thirsty for our love. He becomes a beggar at our door. He looks for generous souls but He tells me that He does not find enough sincere souls. Jesus does not ask from us heavy things. He says:

If you only knew how I am ready to forgive your era's crimes by just one kind look at Me, a moment's regret, a sigh of hesitation, a slight reconsideration, a smile at My Holy Face and I shall forgive and forget. I shall not even look at My Wounds.

Today Jesus is not loved. Not really. And those who love Him truly are very few. He comes to me to complain how unloved He is, how misunderstood, mocked and jeered upon He is. On October 21, 1992, Jesus said to me:

I have allowed your soul to stretch out and touch Me, what have you felt? What did your fingertips feel around My Heart? Petals of roses? No? Then what did you feel? Different bouquets of chosen flowers? Oh no, those who receive bouquets of flowers are loved. Then what did your hands feel? Thorns? Yes! and much more than a crown of thorns: you have felt the lance's blade...I want you to expiate for all those who offend Me and wound Me.—NB 63:13–14

Jesus asks all of us to make real sacrifices and offer them to Him. On the 30th March, 1992, Jesus says:

I need sacrificial love. How many are ready to sacrifice?...Will the ear of anyone yield to My supplica-

*tions?...I am kind and ever so compassionate but very
few want to be in union with Me. Who will give away
his motives for My Motives? Who is willing to give up
his interests for Mine? Who will seek what is least
sought in this world and bear it with love? —My
Cross— and who is ready to seek what is least sought
among you, who will seek: Love?*—NB 58:63–64

Jesus suffers when souls are cold, arid, and like a
desert, but rejoices when a soul is like a garden, even
more, when it is like a heaven for Him.

The Prayer Without Ceasing

If you knew how much Jesus rejoices when we consider Him and make Him our Holy Companion! How
much He loves it when we do not forget Him but speak
to Him all through the day and share our day with Him!
It is the prayer without ceasing and from the heart
which He insists on all the time.

The prayer without ceasing and from the heart means
to be awake. To be awake is to be aware of God's
Presence. And to be aware of God's Presence is to be in
God; it is to be living a: TRUE LIFE IN GOD.

Jesus Feels Our Actions Mystically

One day, while being under His dictation, I was
seeing Jesus with the eyes of my soul, sitting near me.
In front of me I had a statue of the Sacred Heart. While

He was speaking, I suddenly bent towards the Sacred Heart statue and kissed it on the right cheek. Simultaneously, I saw the real Jesus quickly put His Hand on His right cheek, just there where I had kissed Him on His statue and He had an astonished, pure, childish look, and He looked so happy!

I learned that, mystically, somehow, Jesus feels our gestures and intention on His images. For example, once back in Bangladesh, while I was in dictation with the Lord, I was now and then looking at the picture of the Shroud. Somehow, with a gesture done by my mind, I pushed His hair from his Face. He abruptly stopped His dictation and said quickly: "I felt your hand!" I was very surprised, and, thinking I had offended Him, I apologized. But He quickly made me understand that I had not at all offended Him, just that He felt it.

Before My Conversion
The Precious Key
to Approach Our Heavenly Father

Now I shall go back a few years before my conversion.... If you had told me then, in the beginning of November, 1985 that, after three years, I would be going from nation to nation to be a witness on the love of Christ, I would have laughed in your face, and I would have told you that this could not ever happen to me, not even in my wildest dreams. But as you see, everything is possible for God.

I would like to tell you, even if in every meeting I seem to repeat myself, how God, Our Father, approached me. I believe it is a PRECIOUS KEY for everyone who wants to approach Him and love Him intimately like a little child. We have to become very little and approach Him without fear, without this fear that sometimes takes us far away from our Creator. God tells us that we should not fear Him. We should only fear Him if we rebel against Him. We have to use this PRECIOUS KEY for it opens for us a door to heaven. And if we use it, we will discover that: Intimacy and Simplicity, Patience and Tenderness, Fidelity, Mercy and Infinite Love are the portrait of our Father in Heaven.

But many lost this KEY. This KEY is a means to approach God, because most of the people have made of God a dumb image...a printed word, lifeless on paper...or an intolerant Judge, who condemns without hesitation...in short, we have intellectualized God and we forget that Our Beloved Father in Heaven is the Source of Sublime Love, and that we, we are His offspring. We forget that we come from Him and that we are His seed. We forget that His House is our Home and that He made us heirs of His Kingdom to share His Glory.

Our Eternal Father approached me with these simple words which made such an impact on me that I had the impression that I woke up from a long amnesia. I seemed like a corpse coming back to life. Here are those simple but profound words of His, which are for you, too.

I am your Father. You are mine, you come from Me. You belong to Me. You are loved by Me. Feel loved by Me. You are My seed.

I had difficulties in the beginning understanding God's Love. I had difficulties abandoning myself totally to God. So He took great means that I abandon myself to Him. He made me go through a terrible purification. He made me, all at once, see the state of my soul the way He sees it. What I saw revolted me! It troubled me to the point that I was saying that I do not deserve a normal death, but that one should cut me into small pieces and throw me to the hyenas.

Everyday, with great patience, God, Our Father, waits for our abandonment and our love, but very few are listening and very few are sincere.

God had to convert me first before giving me this mission. His Wisdom first had to teach me to love Him intimately. Without this, God would not have been able to give me this mission. This is why we have to learn to love God intimately, to be able to give Him everything and accept the Cross without the slightest complaint, but instead embrace It with love, because our salvation is only through the Cross.

He asked me to love Him. When I answered Him that I loved Him, He did not reproach me that it was not true, but, with an infinite tenderness, He told me: *"Love Me more."* He then asked me to become intimate with Him and approach Him without fear. God wanted me to understand that, if I did not become intimate with Him and approach Him as a child approaches his father, I would never be able to really love Him with all my heart and soul. Nevertheless, He reminded me that intimacy with Him walks hand in hand with holiness. What He wanted me to understand was that I should never forget that He is Holy. Once we join the two together in the same level, our spirit will cry out to Him: ABBA!

Our Father in Heaven taught me to speak to Him intimately, just like a child speaks to his Dad. He taught me that all prayers said from the heart are heard by Him because they are sincere. He taught me that simple words, simple conversations with Him, are cherished by Him and they appear like priceless jewels.

He revealed to me His Goodness, and, in revealing to me His Goodness, He reveals it to everyone in these messages. For these messages, coming from His Own Mouth, are not just for me. He is not speaking to me alone, but is speaking to you, too.

He speaks to the whole world. He speaks to lay people and to priests, to converts and non-converts, to the religious, to the pagans, to the just and to the unjust. He speaks to the ones who love Him and to those who hate Him. He speaks to all His creatures for we all belong to Him since we are His Seed. And since we all come from Him and He loves each one of us with an Eternal Love, we, too, must love one another as He loves us, since He loves every soul. For we will be grieving Him and going against His Law if we would not love one another.

This was what I wanted to tell you about our Heavenly Father. To conclude this witnessing about our Father, I will read to you a passage taken from these messages, so that I make you understand how much we are neglecting Our Father.

Presents and gifts I do not receive many, tell them that Yahweh, your Eternal Father, Father of all, asks them to seek His Face now and then.—NB

Grace Does Not Go Without the Cross—

The Persecutions

I tell you, if the Lord had not come, Himself, to fetch me and convert me, I bet you that I would be still, to this day, wandering and unaware of His Presence and of His Love He has for each one of us.

He came to fetch me Himself, and on top of this He came to instruct me in an extraordinary way, becoming my personal Educator and Teacher. He gave me the charisma to be able to see Him with the eyes of my soul and hear Him interiorly. All this was given me so as to give it, also, to you and to prepare me for this mission.

If the Lord had not allowed me to touch His Heart and make me witness the Riches within it, and if He had not bestowed on me innumerable favors, I should not have had the courage nor the strength to continue in peace and with perseverance the work He has given me.

I would not have endured either the trials, the oppositions, the false witnesses, the criticism or the assaults of the devil, if God did not walk before me.

When I am persecuted I say to myself: I am only the instrument that God chose for this Work which is not my work. They are persecuting the Works of God, not me, so why should I fear? God is most Powerful and Omnipotent. I have not sought this mission, nor have I sought this Way either, so I have no hand in the matter. I am just doing what He wants me to do. I am obeying God. AND NOBODY would be able to defeat God. NOBODY would succeed to suppress His Voice.

As for the mouths that calumniate me, they are facilitating my way to heaven, and are only making my compensation in heaven all the greater. Therefore, it is really a service they are rendering me.

So nobody will succeed to take away this Peace that the Lord has given me, no calumnies, nor persecutions, nor false witnesses nor the fury of the devil!...Praised be Jesus!

Many times our Lord tells me: *"Rejoice! when they are calumniating you! See what a favor I am granting you?"* Or, *"See how generous I am with you?"* And on August 6, 1991:

> *You are hounded for My Sake. Do not fear, I am near you and by your side to encourage you.—You are condemned, but it is only by the world.—For My Sake you are disgraced by human lip. <u>Rejoice!</u> for <u>I</u> was too! Have I not said that no man is greater than His Master? You are the jest of your people, but so was I, your King. When they scourge you on the Way to Calvary, your blood will mingle with Mine. What better favor can I offer you than making out of you another live crucifix for My Glory?—NB 53:35–36*

We Have to Decide for God
and Allow Him to Reign in Us

Our Lord and Our Blessed Mother call us all to conversion.

Therefore, we have to decide for God. There is no other way. We have to decide to abandon ourselves to God completely and to allow His Spirit to transfigure us according to His desires.

We must, therefore, die to our egoism, die to ourselves, so that His Spirit could breathe in us and have space to act. When I say space, I mean by this that as long as we are filled with ourselves, we will be continuing to fight and suppress the Holy Spirit. We really have to decide to put God first. We should allow God to possess us and root Himself in us. We should long to treasure like a pearl His Kingdom. We should allow Christ to reign in us. We should allow Christ to place His Throne in His Dwelling Place that is our soul.

He will establish His Kingdom in a poor and simple soul to reign. Has he not said:

"How happy are the poor in spirit; theirs is the Kingdom of Heaven." (Mt. 5:3). Jesus wants to reign in us for our salvation.

How I long to give you all that God has given me in His Goodness! If you only knew how wonderful is His Love for us! God loves each one of us as if no one else existed around. A unique love! If only you could penetrate in this Love of His, you would be then living for Him alone. You would love Him without self-interest.

And today what He is trying to teach us is again for our salvation.

On the other hand, as long as we are not reconciled with one another we are still at war with God. Many are still on the way to war, even if they call themselves converts, for they have not really reconciled with one another. So as long as we do not abandon ourselves to God, we are not in peace with God. The reflection of this is the wars in our countries. What we carry in our hearts is reflected outside.

This is what the Lord says on the 14th September, 1992:

> *Explain then to Me why every time I speak of recon-ciliation you turn your eyes away from Me...I was a stranger and you did not welcome Me, I was at your door knocking and you did not hear Me; though I have spoken the Truth, your tongue never ceased to tell foul lies about Me, judging Me and condemning Me; ...I visited you with love and tenderness with a yearning to unite you all in My Heart and teach you all over again the rules of My primitive church, but you allowed your own rules to invade your spirit, throwing Me out of your heart.*—NB 62:9–11

Jesus means that what we do to the least we do it to Him.

The Devil's Tactics

Learn that the devil does his utmost to divide us and keep us divided. The devil rejoices every time he succeeds to tear on Christ's Body. This is why we should never give the devil a foothold to tear onChrist's Body. To divide us the devil will use two things before he acts. He will create misunderstandings and confusions out of nothing, that would lead to disputes to bring you where he wants: DIVISION. Thus tearing the Body of Christ again and again.

Therefore, when anyone senses there is a confusion, let us be wise so that we do not allow the devil to lead us into the second step, which is disputes, that definitively will lead us into division.

If you ask: "How am I to avoid this?" The answer to all of us is this:

**LET US PRAY WITH THE HEART
LET US FORGIVE WITH OUR HEART
LET US LOVE ONE ANOTHER
AS GOD LOVES US
LET US BE PERFECT
LIKE OUR FATHER IN HEAVEN IS PERFECT!**